Macmillan McGraw-Hill

California Mathematics 5

Reteach and Skills Practice

Mc Graw Hill Macmillan McGraw-Hill

TO THE STUDENT   This *Reteach and Skills Practice Workbook* gives you additional examples and problems for the concept exercises in each lesson. The exercises are designed to help you study mathematics by reinforcing important skills needed to succeed in the everyday world. The materials are organized by chapter and lesson, with one Reteach and Skills Practice worksheet for every lesson in *California Mathematics, Grade 5*.

Always keep your workbook handy. Along with you textbook, daily homework, and class notes, the completed *Reteach and Skills Practice Workbook* can help you in reviewing for quizzes and tests.

TO THE TEACHER   These worksheets are the same ones found in the Chapter Resource Masters for *California Mathematics, Grade 5*. The answers to these worksheets are available at the end of each Chapter Resource Masters booklet.

Macmillan McGraw-Hill

The *McGraw·Hill* Companies

Send all inquiries to:
Macmillan/McGraw-Hill
8787 Orion Place
Columbus, OH 43240

ISBN: 978-0-02-106347-5
MHID: 0-02-106347-8

Reteach and Skills Practice Workbook, Grade 5

Printed in the United States of America

10 11 12 13 14 15 16 17 MAL 19 18 17 16 15 14 13 12

Contents

Chapter 8 Algebra: Ratios and Functions

Chapter 9 Percent

Chapter 10 Geometry: Angles and Polygons

Chapter 11 Measurement: Perimeter, Area, and Volume

Name _____   Date _____

Reteach

Prime Factors

You can make a factor tree to find the prime factors of a number. Here are two factor trees that show the prime factors of 24.

• A **prime** number has exactly two factors, 1 and itself.

• A **composite** number is a number greater than 1 with more than two factors.

• **0** and **1** are neither prime nor composite.

You get the same prime factors each way.

$24 = 2 \times 2 \times 2 \times 3$ ⟵ prime factorization

Tell whether each number is *prime*, *composite*, or *neither*. Find the prime factorization for the composite numbers.

1. 15

_____

_____

2. 45

_____

_____

3. 7

_____

_____

4. 25

_____

_____

5. 90

_____

_____

6. 11

_____

_____

Name _____ Date _____

Skills Practice

Prime Factors

Use a factor tree to find the prime factors of each number.

1.   48
      8 × 6
   2 × 4 × 2 × 3
   _____

2.   56
      7 × 8
   7 × 4 × 2
   _____

3.   36
      6 × 6
   _____

Find the prime factorization of each number. Tell whether each number is *prime*, *composite*, or *neither*.

4. 1

_____

_____

5. 45

_____

_____

6. 18

_____

_____

7. 23

_____

_____

8. 39

_____

_____

9. 55

_____

_____

10. 28

_____

_____

11. 79

_____

_____

12. 62

_____

_____

Solve.

13. There are 24 students in Mrs. Green's class. The number of boys and the number of girls are both prime numbers. There are 2 more boys than girls. How many boys and how many girls are in the class?

_____

Name _____ Date _____

Reteach

Order of Operations

You can use a phrase to help you remember the order of operations.

Please	**E**xcuse	**M**y	**D**ear	**A**unt	**S**ally
Parentheses	**E**xponents	**M**ultiply	**D**ivide	**A**dd	**S**ubtract

Evaluate.		$8^2 + (6 - 2) \times 5 - 10 \div 2$
Step 1	**P**arentheses	$8^2 + \mathbf{4} \times 5 - 10 \div 2$
Step 2	**E**xponents	$\mathbf{64} + 4 \times 5 - 10 \div 2$
Step 3	**M**ultiply and **D**ivide from left to right.	$64 + \mathbf{20} - \mathbf{5}$
Step 4	**A**dd and **S**ubtract from left to right.	**79**

Find the value of each expression. Follow the steps in the order of operations.

1. $6^2 - 10 + 5 \times (2 - 1)$

$6^2 - 10 + 5 \times$ _____

_____ $- 10 + 5 \times$ _____

_____ $- 10 +$ _____ $=$ _____

2. $6 \times (9 - 4) + 3^2$

$6 \times$ _____ $+ 3^2$

$6 \times$ _____ $+$ _____

_____ $+$ _____ $=$ _____

Find the value of each expression.

3. $7 \times (3 + 9) =$ _____

4. $(12 + 3) - 2 + 3 \times 7 =$ _____

5. $3 \times 4^2 + 8 - 5 =$ _____

6. $100 + 10^2 \times (6 - 3) =$ _____

7. $36 \times 3 - 10 =$ _____

8. $5^2 \times 2 + 4 =$ _____

9. $6^2 \div (9 - 5) + 7 =$ _____

10. $25 - 2 \times 6 + 4^2 =$ _____

11. $9 \times (14 - 3) \div 3 =$ _____

12. $63 \div 9 + 2 \times 5 =$ _____

Name _____ Date _____

Skills Practice

Order of Operations

Find the value of each expression.

1. $44 + 7 \times 3$ _____

2. $48 \div (8 - 2)$ _____

3. $(3 + 4) \times 8 \div 2$ _____

4. $18 + 12 \div 2 + 3$ _____

5. $4^2 \times 2 - 10$ _____

6. $(6 \div 3) + (8 \times 5)$ _____

7. $(3 + 2) \times 3^2$ _____

8. $24 \div 6 \times 3 + 52$ _____

9. $(2 \times 5) - (3 \times 3)$ _____

10. $96 \div (3 \times 4) \div 2$ _____

11. $100 - 8^2 + 4 \div 4$ _____

12. $(200 - 50) \div (12 - 9)$ _____

13. $47 + 3 \times 11 - 36 \div 3$ _____

14. $(7 + 6) \times (7 - 3)$ _____

15. $50 - (-4 + 1)^2 \div 9$ _____

16. $6^2 - 9 \times 4 + (1 + 2)^2$ _____

Solve.

17. Tickets to the school play cost $4 for adults and $2 for students. If 255 adults and 382 students attended the play, write an expression that shows the total amount of money made on ticket sales. Then simplify the expression.

_____

_____

18. At the school play, popcorn costs $1 and juice costs $2. Suppose 235 people buy popcorn and 140 people buy juice. Write an expression that shows the total amount of money made by selling refreshments. Then simplify the expression.

_____

Name _____ Date _____

Reteach

Problem-Solving Investigation

The three tallest buildings in Boston are the Prudential Tower (750 ft), the John Hancock Tower (790 ft), and the Federal Reserve Building (604 ft). How much taller is the Prudential Tower than the Federal Reserve Building?

Step 1 **Understand**	**Be sure you understand the problem.** Read carefully. Identify what you need to do. • What do you know? _____ • What have you been asked to do? _____
Step 2 **Plan**	You can subtract the heights of the buildings. **Plan a strategy.** • Decide what actions you will take and in what order.
Step 3 **Solve**	**Solve the problem.** Follow your plan. Subtract the height of the Federal Reserve Building from the height of the Prudential Tower. $\begin{array}{r} 7\overset{4}{\cancel{5}}\overset{10}{\cancel{0}} \\ -\ 604 \\ \hline 146 \end{array}$ Prudential Tower is 146 feet taller than the Federal Reserve Building.
Step 4 **Check**	**Did you answer the question? Is the solution reasonable?** Yes, you have found the difference in heights.

Solve. Use the four-step process.

1. Scotia Plaza in Toronto is 902 feet tall. First Canadian Place in Toronto is 978 feet tall. How much taller is First Canadian Place than Scotia Plaza?

   _____

   _____

2. Dallas' Renaissance Tower is 886 feet, Bank of America Plaza is 921 feet, and Comerica Bank Tower is 787 feet. What is the total height of all 3 buildings?

   _____

Name _____ Date _____

Reteach

Problem-Solving Investigation (continued)

3. The Andersons are buying a paddle boat for $530. They plan to pay in four equal payments. How much will their payments be?

_____

4. Lynn can walk two miles in 24 minutes. At this rate, how long will it take her to walk 6 miles?

_____

5. Bridgit plays on the basketball team. The table shows the number of baskets she made in the first six days of practice. If the pattern continues, how many baskets will she make on the eighth day?

Day	Baskets
1	21
2	22
3	24
4	27
5	31
6	36
7	
8	

_____

6. The Glendale Plaza Building in Glendale, California is 353 feet tall. The U.S. Bank Tower in Los Angeles, California is 1,017 feet tall. Which building is taller?

_____

7. After going on vacation, you come home with $5. You spent $6 on a pair of sunglasses, $10 on snacks, $4 on a book, and $5 on arcade games. How much money did you start with?

_____

Name _____ Date _____

Skills Practice
Problem-Solving Investigation

Solve. Use the four-step plan.

1. The three highest mountains in Colorado are Mount Massive (14,421 ft), Mount Harvard (14,420 ft), and Mount Elbert (14,433 ft). How much taller is Mount Elbert than Mount Massive?

_____

2. Hoover Dam, in the United States, is 223 meters high. Ertan Dam, in China, is 240 meters high. In Canada, Mica Dam is 243 meters high. What is the total height of all three dams?

_____

3. The Akshi Kaikyo suspension bridge in Japan has a span of 6,570 feet. The Humber suspension bridge in England has a span of 4,626 feet. How much longer is the Humber suspension bridge than the Akshi Kaikyo suspension bridge?

_____

4. There are three long tunnels that go under Boston Harbor. The Sumner Tunnel is 5,653 feet long. The Callahan Tunnel is 5,070 feet long. The Ted Williams Tunnel is 8,448 feet long. What is the total length of all three tunnels?

_____

Use the data from the table for problems 5–6.

Land Tunnels in the United States		
Tunnel	State	Length (ft)
Liberty Tubes	Pennsylvania	5,920
Devil's Side	California	3,400
E. Johnson Memorial	Colorado	8,959
Squirrel Hill	Pennsylvania	4,225

6. How much longer is the longest tunnel than Devil's Side tunnel?

_____

5. Which tunnel is the longest?

_____

1–5

Reteach

Algebra: Variables and Expressions

A box contains some baseballs. There are 2 baseballs on the ground. How many baseballs are there altogether?

You can draw models to show the total number of baseballs if the box contains certain numbers of baseballs.

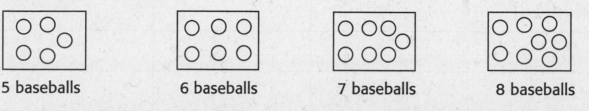

| 5 baseballs | 6 baseballs | 7 baseballs | 8 baseballs |

You can also write an algebraic expression to represent the total number of baseballs.

- The number of baseballs in the box changes, so represent it with the variable, b.

- The number of baseballs on the ground stays the same: 2.

- Add the number of baseballs in the box and the number on the ground to find the number of baseballs altogether.

So, $b + 2$ represents the total number of baseballs.

Suppose there are 9 baseballs in the box. $b = 9$
You can find the total number of baseballs $b + 2$
by evaluating the expression. $9 + 2 = 11$ baseballs

Complete the steps to write and evaluate an expression for the situation.

1. Laura had 5 more hits than Susan. How many hits did Laura have?

   What number changes? _____

   Write a variable to represent the number that changes. _____

   What number stays the same? _____

   Write the number that stays the same. _____

   What operation do you need to use to find the number of hits Laura had? _____

   Write an expression to represent the number of hits Laura had. _____

   Suppose Susan had 2 hits. Evaluate the expression. _____

2. The Mustangs scored m runs in the softball game. The Rangers scored 3 fewer runs than the Mustangs. How many runs did the Rangers get?

3. During the softball season, the Rangers won y games. They lost 4 more games than they won. How many games did the Rangers lose during the season?

_____   _____

Name _____ Date _____

Skills Practice

Algebra: Variables and Expressions

Complete the table.

Algebraic Expressions	Variables	Numbers	Operations
1. $3 + m$			
2. $8x - 3$			
3. $5d + 2c$			

Evaluate each expression if $a = 3$ and $b = 4$.

4. $b + 8$ _____   **5.** $a + b$ _____   **6.** $b - a$ _____

7. $10 + b$ _____   **8.** $2a$ _____   **9.** $4b$ _____

10. $a \times b$ _____   **11.** $7a \times 9b$ _____   **12.** $8a - 9$ _____

13. $b \times 2$ _____   **14.** $a + 1$ _____   **15.** $18 \div 2a$ _____

16. $a^2 \times b^2$ _____   **17.** $ab \div 3$ _____   **18.** $15a - 4b$ _____

Evaluate each expression if $x = 7$, $y = 15$, and $z = 8$.

19. $x + y + z$ _____   **20.** $x + 2z$ _____   **21.** xz _____

22. $4x$ _____   **23.** $z \div 4$ _____   **24.** $6z - 5$ _____

25. $9y$ _____   **26.** x^2 _____   **27.** $y + 4 \times 6$ _____

28. y^2 _____   **29.** $x^2 + 30$ _____   **30.** $zx \div 4$ _____

Name _____ Date _____

Reteach

5AF1.2, 5AF1.5

Algebra: Functions

A **function rule** describes the relationship between the input and output of a **function**. The inputs and outputs can be organized in a **function table**.

Example 1 **Complete the function table.**

The function rule is $x - 3$. So, subtract 3 from each input.

Input (x)	$x - 3$	Output
9	$9 - 3$	■
8	$8 - 3$	■
6	$6 - 3$	■

→

Input (x)	Output ($x - 3$)
9	6
8	5
6	3

Example 2 **Find the rule for the function table.**

Input (x)	Output (■)
0	0
1	4
2	8

Study the relationship between each input and output.

Input	Output
$0 \times 4 \rightarrow 0$	
$1 \times 4 \rightarrow 4$	
$2 \times 4 \rightarrow 8$	

The output is four times the input. So, the function rule is $4x$.

Complete each function table.

1.

Input (x)	Output ($2x$)
0	
2	
4	

2.

Input (x)	Output ($4 + x$)
0	
1	
4	

3.

Input (x)	Output (■)
1	3
2	4
5	7

4.

Input (x)	Output (■)
2	1
6	3
10	5

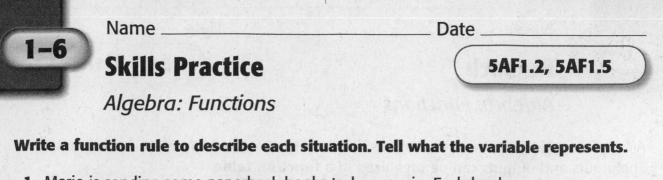

Write a function rule to describe each situation. Tell what the variable represents.

1. Marie is sending some paperback books to her cousin. Each book weighs 4 ounces. She is mailing them in a box that weighs 6 ounces.

   Variable: _____

   Function Rule: _____

Complete the table. Then write a function rule to describe the situation. Tell what the variable represents.

2. Steven is ordering puzzles for his friends. It costs $12.50 to buy the first one and it costs $7.50 for each additional puzzle.

Number of Puzzles	1	2	3	4	5
Total Cost	$12.50	$20.00	$27.50		

   Variable: _____

   _____

   Function Rule: _____

Use the information below to solve problems 3–4.

It takes Beth 20 minutes to drive to and from a mailing service and 2 minutes to fill out a mailing label and have each package weighed.

3. Write a function rule to describe the situation. Tell what the variable represents.

   _____

   _____

4. How long will it take Beth to mail 3 packages? Use the rule you wrote to solve the problem.

   _____

1–7

Reteach

5MR2.6, 4NS2.1

Problem-Solving Strategy

Guess and Check

During summer vacation, Sanjay buys keychains and postcards for his friends at home. A keychain costs $3, and a postcard costs $1. Sanjay buys gifts for 8 friends and spends $12. How many keychains and postcards did he buy?

Step 1 Understand	**Be sure you understand the problem.**
	Read carefully. Identify what you need to do.
	What facts do you know?
	• A keychain costs _____ and a postcard costs _____.
	• Sanjay buys _____ gifts.
	• He spends _____.
	What do you need to find?
	• The number of _____.
Step 2 Plan • Use Logical Reasoning • Draw a Diagram • Make a Graph • Make a Table or List • Find a Pattern • Guess and Check	**Make a plan.** Choose a strategy. You can solve the problem by making a guess. Then check the guess. If it is not the correct answer, adjust the guess and check again until you find the correct answer.

Step 3 Solve	**Follow your plan.** Make a guess about the number of keychains and the number of postcards. Suppose you guess 4 keychains and 4 postcards. Check the amounts for the guess. Keychains: _____ × _____ = _____ Postcards: _____ × _____ = _____ Total Cost: _____ + _____ = _____ Does the guess check with the total that Sanjay spent? _____ Should you adjust the number of keychains up or down? Explain. _____ _____ Adjust your guess. Check your guess. Did the guess check? _____ If your guess did not check, adjust it again. How many keychains did Sanjay buy? _____ How many postcards did Sanjay buy? _____
Step 4 Check	**Look back. Did you answer the question?** Is the solution reasonable? Reread the problem. Have you answered the question? _____ How can you check your answer? _____ _____

Practice

1. Nelson has 7 paper bills. All the bills are $1 and $5. He has a total of $15. How many $1 bills and how many $5 bills does he have?

_____

2. The library charges 25¢ a day for overdue videos and 5¢ a day for overdue books. Emily returns a video and a book that were due on the same day, and pays a total of 90¢ in late fees. How many days late were her items?

_____

Name _____ Date _____

Skills Practice

Problem-Solving Strategy

Use the guess-and-check strategy to solve.

1. The Bactrian camel has two humps and the Dromedary camel has one hump. In a group of 15 camels, the total number of humps is 21. How many camels of each type are there?

_____

2. The circus orders bicycles and unicycles for a new act. It orders a total of 12 cycles. The cycles have 16 tires altogether. How many bicycles and unicycles did the circus order?

_____

3. Anja buys a magazine and a pizza. She spends $8.10. The magazine costs $2.40 less than the pizza. How much does the pizza cost?

_____

4. A letter to Europe from the United States costs $0.94 to mail. A letter mailed within the United States costs $0.42. Nancy mails 5 letters for $3.14, some to Europe and some to the United States. How many letters did she send to Europe?

_____

Use any strategy to solve.

5. Warren spent $8.50 at the store. He spent $2.40 on paper, $0.88 on pencils, and $2.65 on markers. He spent the rest on a notebook. How much did the notebook cost?

_____

Strategy: _____

6. Ms. Baxter takes a group of 8 children to a concert. Tickets for children 12 years and older cost $3. Tickets for children under 12 cost $2. She spends a total of $19 on tickets for the children. How many children are 12 and older?

_____

Strategy: _____

Name _____ Date _____

Reteach

Algebra: Equations

An **equation** is a sentence that contains an **equals sign**, =. Sometimes equations contain variables and we need to solve for the variable.

Equation	Equation Containing a Variable
$3 + 4 = 7$	$3 + x = 7$

When you replace a variable with a number that makes the sentence true, you **solve** the equation. The **solution** of the equation is the value of the variable.

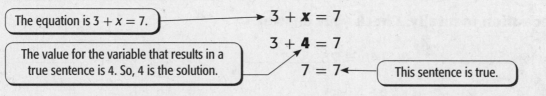

The equation is $3 + x = 7$. $\longrightarrow$ $3 + \mathbf{x} = 7$

The value for the variable that results in a true sentence is 4. So, 4 is the solution. $3 + \mathbf{4} = 7$

$7 = 7 \longleftarrow$ This sentence is true.

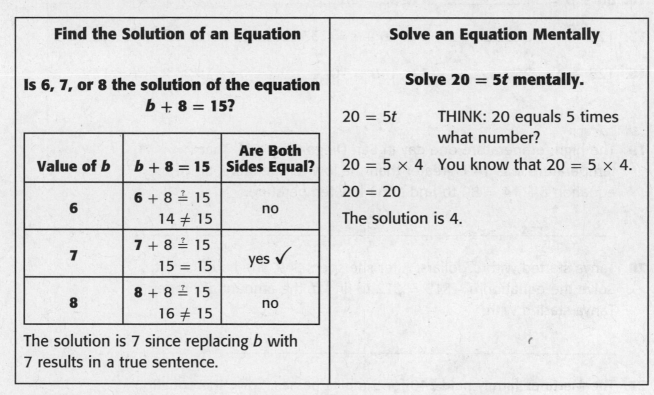

	Find the Solution of an Equation	

Is 6, 7, or 8 the solution of the equation $b + 8 = 15$?

Value of b	$b + 8 = 15$	Are Both Sides Equal?
6	$6 + 8 \overset{?}{=} 15$ $14 \neq 15$	no
7	$7 + 8 \overset{?}{=} 15$ $15 = 15$	yes ✓
8	$8 + 8 \overset{?}{=} 15$ $16 \neq 15$	no

The solution is 7 since replacing b with 7 results in a true sentence.

Solve an Equation Mentally

Solve $20 = 5t$ mentally.

$20 = 5t$ THINK: 20 equals 5 times what number?

$20 = 5 \times 4$ You know that $20 = 5 \times 4$.

$20 = 20$

The solution is 4.

Identify the solution of each equation from the list given.

1. $6 + c = 18$; 11, 12, 13 _____

2. $9 \div w = 3$; 3, 4, 5 _____

Solve each equation mentally.

3. $10j = 40$ _____

4. $45 = 5b$ _____

Name _____ Date _____

Skills Practice

Algebra: Equations

Identify the solution of each equation from the list given.

1. $3 + f = 12$; 7, 8, 9

2. $6g = 36$; 6, 7, 8

3. $8 - c = 2$; 5, 6, 7

_____ _____ _____

4. $3b = 30$; 10, 11, 12

5. $18 \div x = 3$; 4, 5, 6

6. $12 + z = 29$; 15, 16, 17

_____ _____ _____

Solve each equation mentally. Check your answer.

7. $13 - g = 12$ _____

8. $14h = 28$ _____

9. $21 - v = 16$ _____

10. $88 \div p = 11$ _____

11. $9k = 36$ _____

12. $19 - e = 7$ _____

13. $123 - r = 88$ _____

14. $78 + s = 133$ _____

15. $8d = 72$ _____

16. $125 \div p = 25$ _____

17. $14u = 70$ _____

18. $33 \div d = 11$ _____

19. The high temperature one day in San Diego was 80°F. That temperature was 14°F greater than the low temperature. Solve the equation $t + 14 = 80$ to find t, the low temperature.

_____

20. Tanya started with d dollars. After she spent \$19, she had \$12 left. Solve the equation $d - \$19 = \$12$ to find d, the amount of money Tanya started with.

_____

21. The Martinez family paid \$40 for 5 movie passes. Solve the equation $5c = \$40$ to find the cost in dollars, c, of each movie pass.

_____

22. Three friends split the cost of a gift equally. Each paid \$4. Solve $t \div 3 = \$4$ to find t, the cost in dollars of the gift.

_____

Name _____ Date _____

Reteach

5AF1.2, 5MG1.4

Algebra: Area Formulas

Area is the number of square units needed to cover the inside of a region or plane figure. To find the area of a rectangle or square, you can multiply its length times its width. This can be shown by a formula.

Find the area of the rectangle.
Use the formula $A = lw$, where A = area, l = length, and w = width.

13 in.

4 in.

$A = lw$

$A = 13 \times 4$

$A = 52$ square inches

Find the area of the square.
Use the formula $A = s^2$, where A = area and s = length of a side.

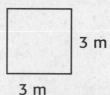

3 m

3 m

$A = s^2$

$A = 3 \times 3$

$A = 9$ square meters

Find the area of each rectangle.

1.

5 in.

7 in.

$A = lw$

$A = $ _____ × _____

$A = $ _____ square inches

2.

5 ft

5 ft

$A = s^2$

$A = $ _____ × _____

$A = $ _____ square feet

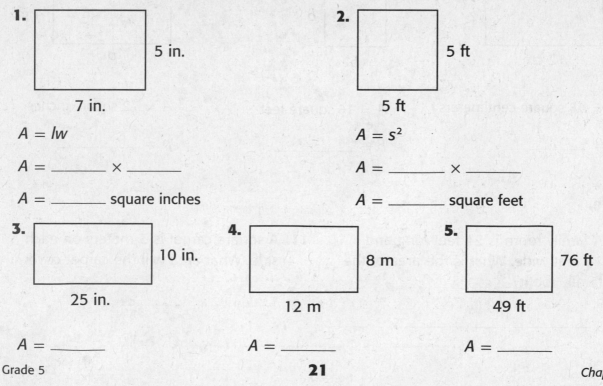

3.

10 in.

25 in.

4.

8 m

12 m

5.

76 ft

49 ft

$A = $ _____

$A = $ _____

$A = $ _____

Name _____ Date _____

Skills Practice

Algebra: Area Formulas

Find the area of each rectangle.

1.

4 in.

8 in.

A = _____

2.

16 cm

21 cm

A = _____

3.

9 ft

9 ft

A = _____

4.

3 cm

3 cm

A = _____

5.

6 cm

1 cm

A = _____

6.

25 in.

25 in.

A = _____

Find each missing measurement.

7.

z

12 cm

A = 48 square centimeters

z = _____

8.

b

b

A = 16 square feet

b = _____

9.

4 in.

p

A = 72 square inches

p = _____

Solve.

10. A family room is 24 feet long and 18 feet wide. What is the area of the family room?

_____

11. A square carpet is 3 meters on each side. What area will the carpet cover?

_____

Name _____ Date _____

Reteach

Algebra: The Distributive Property

You can use place-value models to show the Distributive Property.

Multiply 3 × 26.

Multiply and add (3 × 20) + (3 × 6).

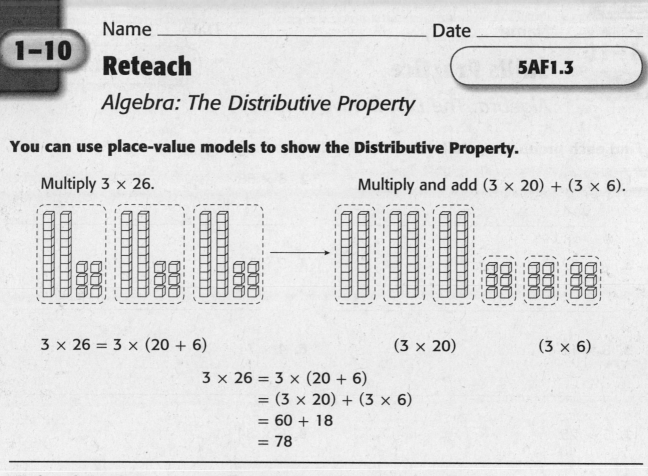

$3 \times 26 = 3 \times (20 + 6)$

(3×20)

(3×6)

$$3 \times 26 = 3 \times (20 + 6)$$
$$= (3 \times 20) + (3 \times 6)$$
$$= 60 + 18$$
$$= 78$$

Find each product. You can draw place-value models to help you multiply.

1. $5 \times 39 = 5 \times ($ _____ + _____ $)$

    $= (5 \times$ _____ $) + (5 \times$ _____ $)$

    $=$ _____ + _____

    $=$ _____

2. $8 \times 46 = 8 \times ($ _____ + _____ $)$

    $= (8 \times$ _____ $) + (8 \times$ _____ $)$

    $=$ _____ + _____

    $=$ _____

3. $3 \times 54 =$ _____ $\times ($ ___ + ___ $)$

    $= ($ ___ × ___ $) + ($ ___ × ___ $)$

    $=$ _____ + _____

    $=$ _____

4. $6 \times 64 =$ _____ $\times ($ ___ + ___ $)$

    $= ($ ___ × ___ $) + ($ ___ × ___ $)$

    $=$ _____ + _____

    $=$ _____

5. $2 \times 48 =$ _____

6. $4 \times 72 =$ _____

7. $9 \times 27 =$ _____

8. $7 \times 45 =$ _____

Name _____ Date _____

Skills Practice

Algebra: The Distributive Property

Find each product mentally. Use the Distributive Property.

1. 3×13

2. 8×68

_____ _____

3. 7×32

4. 9×35

_____ _____

5. 8×17

6. 4×71

_____ _____

7. 5×25

8. 6×84

_____ _____

Rewrite each expression using the Distributive Property.

9. $7 \times 19 =$ _____ **10.** $6 \times 22 =$ _____ **11.** $8 \times 58 =$ _____

12. $5 \times 13 =$ _____ **13.** $4 \times 76 =$ _____ **14.** $2 \times 27 =$ _____

15. $9 \times 56 =$ _____ **16.** $3 \times 71 =$ _____ **17.** $7 \times 33 =$ _____

18. $8 \times 34 =$ _____ **19.** $4 \times 83 =$ _____ **20.** $3 \times 27 =$ _____

21. $6 \times 88 =$ _____ **22.** $9 \times 98 =$ _____ **23.** $5 \times 65 =$ _____

24. $5 \times 36 =$ _____ **25.** $3 \times 98 =$ _____ **26.** $2 \times 97 =$ _____

2-1

Reteach

5SDAP1.2

Bar Graphs and Line Graphs

A **bar graph** is used to compare categories of data. The categories are written on the horizontal axis. The scale, which is separated into equal parts or intervals, is written on the vertical axis.

A **line graph** is used to show how a data set changes over a period of time. The time interval is shown on the horizontal axis. The scale is written on the vertical axis.

Use the graphs to complete each statement.

Club Members at Middle School

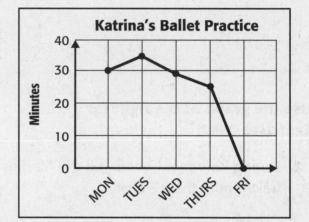

1. This is a _____ graph.

2. The interval of club members is _____ members.

3. According to the graph, the most popular club is _____.

4. This is a _____ graph.

5. The interval of time is _____.

6. According to the graph, Katrina has no ballet practice on _____.

Name _____ Date _____

Skills Practice

Bar Graphs and Line Graphs

1. The table shows the times Ken rode his bike each day last week. Make a bar graph of the data.

Time Ken Spent Riding a Bike

Day	Minutes
Sunday	20
Monday	30
Tuesday	25
Wednesday	5
Thursday	20
Friday	15
Saturday	30

Use the graph at the right for Exercises 2–4.

2. During how many years did the Martins travel more than 7 days?

   _____

3. In which years did the number of travel days *increase*?

   _____

4. In which years did the number of travel days *decrease*?

   _____

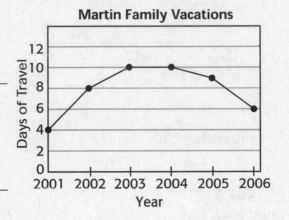

Martin Family Vacations

Name _____ Date _____

Reteach

Interpret Line Graphs

You can use a line graph to show how a quantity changes over time. This graph shows Ricky's height over five years. To make a line graph, plot points to represent the data. Then draw a line to connect the points.

Ricky's Height

Year	Height (in inches)
1998	46
1999	47
2000	49
2001	52
2002	56

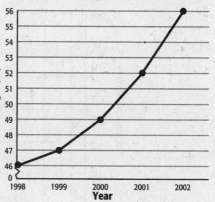

Ricky's Height (in inches)

Marie grew pumpkins. The table shows the weight gain in pounds of one pumpkin. Make a line graph to display the data. Use the line graph to solve the problems.

Marie's Pumpkin

Month	Weight (in pounds)
1	$\frac{1}{2}$
2	1
3	3
4	6
5	$8\frac{1}{2}$
6	9
7	9

1. On a line graph, a line that rises shows that a quantity is increasing. In which months did Marie's pumpkin gain the most weight?

2. On a line graph, a line that is horizontal shows that a quantity stays the same. In which month did the weight of the pumpkin stay the same?

_____   _____

Skills Practice

Interpret Line Graphs

 5SDAP1.4

Sue and Brett each had a lemonade stand. Sue sold pink lemonade and Brett sold regular lemonade. They each charged $0.50 a glass. This double-line graph compares their sales.

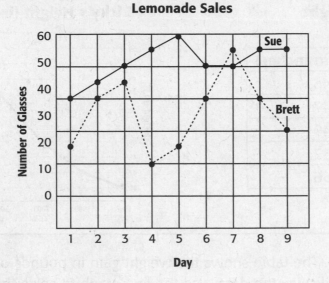

Lemonade Sales

Solve.

1. Who sold more lemonade in nine days? by how many more glasses?

_____

2. After nine days, how much money did Brett earn?

_____

3. In all, how much money did Sue earn?

_____

4. What was the difference in earnings between Sue and Brett?

_____

5. In the next nine days, if Brett sells four times what he sold this time, how many glasses of lemonade will he sell? How much money will he earn?

_____

6. In the next nine days, if Sue sells half the amount she sold during these nine days, how many glasses of lemonade will she sell? How much money will she earn in the next nine days?

_____

28

Name _____ Date _____

Reteach

Histograms

Histograms are similar to bar graphs. They both use bars to display data, but the bars in a histogram are for intervals of data. There are no gaps between the bars of a histogram.

Hikers at Deer Creek Park

Age of Hikers	Number of Hikers
0–10	20
11–20	15
21–30	30
31–40	40
41–50	35

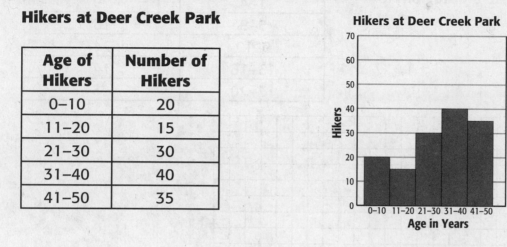

Make a histogram to display the data.

Hikers at Deer Creek Park

Distance in Miles	Number of Hikers
1–3	50
4–6	35
7–9	25
10–12	10
13–15	20

1. What length hike did most hikers take?

_____

2. How many people hiked 10–12 miles?

_____

Name _____ Date _____

Skills Practice

5SDAP1.2

Histograms

1. This table shows the distances people rode their bikes on the Riverside Bike Trail one day. Make a histogram to display the data.

Distances Ridden on Trail

Distance in Miles	Number of Cyclists
1–4	9
5–8	16
9–12	24
13–16	14
17–20	6

Use the data from the histogram at the right for Exercises 2–4.

2. During which time period was the trail the most crowded? The least crowded?

_____

3. Can you tell how many cyclists were on the trail at 5:00 P.M.? Explain.

_____

_____

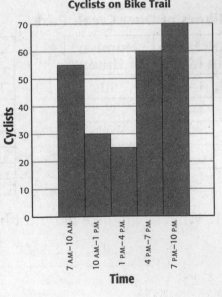

Cyclists on Bike Trail

4. On another day, 3 more cyclists were on the trail at 8 A.M., 5 fewer were on at 2:00 P.M., and 10 more were on at 5:30 P.M. How would the histogram for this day be different?

_____

Name _____ Date _____

Reteach

Line Plots

5SDAP1.2

Students in one fifth-grade class recorded how many first cousins each student had. Here are the results:

6, 5, 1, 7, 3, 4, 4, 5, 1, 5, 6, 4, 7, 5, 5, 6, 7, 5, 4, 6, 4

Make one tally in the frequency table for each time a particular number of first cousins occurs. Count and record the number of tallies. Display the data in a line plot, making one X for each tally.

Frequency Table			Line Plot
Number of First Cousins	**Number of Students**		
	Tally	**Frequency**	
1			
2			
3			
4			
5			
6			
7			

For the next month, the fifth-graders kept a record of how many times they called one of their first cousins on the phone. Here are the results:

2, 0, 2, 1, 1, 3, 4, 2, 2, 3, 4, 3, 6, 0, 3, 2, 1, 2, 3, 1, 2

1. Record the results in the line plot below.

Use the line plot for exercises 2 and 3.

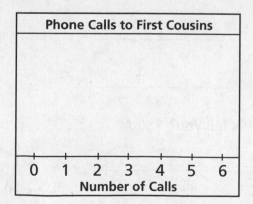

2. How many students made at least one phone call to a first cousin?

_____

3. Sometimes a gap appears in a line plot because a particular result never occurred. Where is the gap in the line plot? What does this tell you?

_____

Name _____ Date _____

Skills Practice

Line Plots

The Johnson family kept a record of the length of telephone calls they made in one weekend.

8 minutes	6 minutes	4 minutes	10 minutes	4 minutes	8 minutes
7 minutes	8 minutes	8 minutes	7 minutes	9 minutes	8 minutes
3 minutes	9 minutes	7 minutes	8 minutes	4 minutes	6 minutes
9 minutes	8 minutes	7 minutes	9 minutes	7 minutes	

1. Record the results in the frequency table below.

Length of Calls in Minutes	Number of Calls	
	Tally	Frequency
3		
4		
5		
6		
7		
8		
9		
10		

2. Make a line plot from the frequency table.

Use data from the line plot for Exercises 3 and 4.

3. Where does most of the data cluster? What does this tell you?

_____

_____

4. Where is the gap in the line plot? What does this tell you?

_____

Name _____ Date _____

Reteach

5MR2.3, 5SDAP1.2

Problem-Solving Strategy

Make a Table

A music store kept track of the number of jazz CDs it sold each week. In how many of the weeks did the number of CDs sold range from 31 to 40?

Number of Jazz CDs Sold					
Week	Number	Week	Number	Week	Number
1	38	6	28	11	17
2	36	7	25	12	15
3	29	8	19	13	18
4	30	9	23	14	21
5	31	10	20	15	23

Step 1 Understand	**What facts do you know?** • The number of _____ **What do you need to find?** • The number of weeks in which _____ _____
Step 2 Plan	**Make a plan.** You can make a table to help you solve the problem. A table can help you organize the data and make it easier to see the totals for each range. Organize the data in ranges. List the number of CDs sold in each range. <table><tr><td>Range</td><td>Number of CDs Sold</td></tr><tr><td>11–20</td><td>19, 20, 17, 15, 18</td></tr><tr><td>21–30</td><td>29, 30, 28, 25, 23, 21, 23</td></tr><tr><td>31–40</td><td>38, 36, 31</td></tr></table>

2-5

Reteach

Problem-Solving Strategy (continued)

Step 3 Solve	**Follow your plan.**

Make a table.

Range	Tall	Frequency
11–20	卌	5
21–30	卌 II	7
31–40	III	3

In how many weeks was the number of CDs sold in the range from 31 to 40?

_____

Step 4 Check	**Is the solution reasonable?**

Look back at the problem.

Does your answer make sense? _____

What other methods could you use to check your answer?

_____

Use the *make a table* strategy to solve.

A meteorologist records the high temperature, in degrees Fahrenheit, each day.

1. How many days did the temperature range from 80°F to 89°F?

   _____

2. How many days did the temperature range from 70°F to 79°F?

   _____

Day	Temperature	Day	Temperature
1	90	6	79
2	86	7	82
3	91	8	76
4	94	9	83
5	88	10	90

2-5

Skills Practice

Problem-Solving Strategy

Use the *make a table* strategy to solve.

A card shop recorded how many packs of trading cards it sold each week.

1. During how many weeks did the number of packs sold range from 30 to 39?

_____

Trading Cards Sold					
Week	**Number of Packs**	**Week**	**Number of Packs**	**Week**	**Number of Packs**
1	28	5	48	9	25
2	32	6	43	10	37
3	38	7	45	11	42
4	44	8	41	12	35

2. How many weeks were 40 or more packs sold?

_____

3. A bookstore recorded 8 months of sales of a particular book. How many months did the number of copies sold range from 20 to 29?

_____

Bookstore Sales			
Month	**Copies**	**Month**	**Copies**
1	26	5	38
2	24	6	19
3	32	7	15
4	18	8	30

4. In a survey, people were asked if they preferred the beach or the mountains for a vacation. How many more people chose the beach over the mountains?

Favorite Vacation Places
B M M M B B M
B B B B B M M B
B B B B M M B B

B = beach

M = mountains

_____

Name _____ Date _____

Reteach

Mean

You can use the mean to describe the average number of fan letters that singer Johnny Jazz received in one week.

Mean = the sum of the numbers divided by the number of addends

Day	Sunday	Monday	Tuesday	Wednesday	Thursday	Friday	Saturday
Number of Fan Letters	17	23	12	15	25	7	13

What you want to know	What you find	How you find it
What is the average number of fan letters received?	total of fan letters ÷ number of days fan letters were received	$17 + 23 + 12 + 15 + 25 + 7 + 13 = 112$ $112 \div 7 = 16$

Find the mean of the following numbers.

1. $88 + 85 + 91$

   _____

2. 255, 134, 313

   _____

3. $79 + 73 + 22$

   _____

4. Yolanda went to the library every day after school for one week. She borrowed 4 books on Monday, 6 on Tuesday, 2 on Wednesday, 4 on Thursday, and 9 on Friday. What is the mean of the books Yolanda borrowed from the library?

   _____

Name _____ Date _____

Skills Practice

Mean

Find the mean to the nearest whole number.

1. 4, 5, 7, 8, 11, 4, 6, 8

_____

2. 13, 12, 11, 7, 9, 15, 5, 5

_____

3. 2, 1, 2, 3, 4, 6, 3

_____

4. 25, 38, 72, 45, 34, 26, 63, 78

_____

5.

Student	Jessie	Angela	Martin	Kara	Taylor	Kristen	Mickey	Julian
Number of Siblings	3	2	1	4	0	1	2	0

_____

Solve.

6. During a week, Bailey drank 4 glasses of water one day, 5 the next, 6 the following day, 7 glasses, 3 glasses, 4 glasses, and finally 5 glasses on the last day of the week. What is the average number of glasses of water Bailey drank a day during those 7 days?

_____

7. Over the course of a year, the monthly rainfall in Water Springs was as follows: 5 in., 7 in., 9 in., 4 in., 9 in., 4 in., 3 in., 5 in., 8 in., 6 in., 3 in., 9 in. What was the average monthly rainfall that year?

_____

Name _____ Date _____

Reteach

5SDAP1.1

Median, Mode, and Range

You can use the range, mode, and median, to describe the numbers of e-mail messages Jon sent.

Number of E-mail Messages Jon Sent							
Day	Sun.	Mon.	Tues.	Wed.	Thur.	Fri.	Sat.
Number of Messages	7	4	6	5	7	5	8

Write the numbers of messages in order from least to greatest.   4, 5, 5, 6, 7, 7, 8

What you want to know	What you find	How you find it
Is there much difference in the numbers of messages sent?	**range** the difference between the greatest and the least number	$8 - 4 = 4$ The range of messages is 4.
What is the most common number of messages sent?	**mode** the number that occurs most often	5 and 7 both appear twice. The other numbers appear once. The mode is 5 and 7 messages.
What is the middle number of messages sent?	**median** the middle number or the average of the two middle numbers	6 is in the middle. The median is 6 messages.

Number of E-mail Messages Jon Received							
Day	Sun.	Mon.	Tues.	Wed.	Thur.	Fri.	Sat.
Number of Messages	3	9	2	5	8	2	6

1. Write the number of messages received in order from least to greatest.

_____

2. What is the greatest number of messages received? The least number?

_____

3. What is the range of messages received? _____

4. What is the mode of messages received? _____

5. What is the median of messages received? _____

Name _____ Date _____

Skills Practice

Median, Mode, and Range

Find the median, mode, and range.

1. 1, 2, 0, 5, 8, 2, 9, 2, 7 _____

2. 9, 4, 7, 9, 3, 10, 8, 6 _____

3. 34, 17, 10, 23, 21, 15 _____

4. 67, 67, 98, 49, 98, 89 _____

5. 27, 31, 76, 59, 33, 48, 24, 58 _____

6. 105, 126, 90, 50, 75, 90, 62, 112 _____

7. $1.50, $2.50, $1.50, $4.00, $5.00 _____

8. 1.2, 1.5, 2.1, 1.7, 3.2, 2.4, 2.8, 1.3 _____

9. 20, 12.5, 30, 15.4, 25, 18.6, 17.8 _____

10. $3.35, $8.50, $3.35, $4.35, $8.25 _____

11.

Student	Ann	Ben	Cara	Fran	Ian	Mike	Kim	Lou
Number of Pets	4	6	0	3	2	5	2	3

_____

Name _____ Date _____

Reteach

Problem-Solving Investigation

Extra or Missing Information

The table shows the number of fifth-graders who signed up for clubs.

How many fifth-graders, total, signed up for a club?

Club	Number of Students
Art	12
Movie	13
Chess	9
Debate	5
None	11

Step 1 Understand	**What do you know?** You know the number of fifth-graders who signed up for each club and the number who signed up for no clubs. **What do you need to find?** You need to find the total number of fifth-graders who signed up for a club.
Step 2 Plan	**Is there any information that is not needed?** The important information is the number of fifth-graders in each club. All other information is unimportant. **Is there any information that is missing?** No.
Step 2 Solve	Fifth-graders in the art club .... 12 Fifth-graders in the movie club .... 13 Fifth-graders in the chess club .... 9 Fifth-graders in the debate club ...... 5 $12 + 13 + 9 + 5 = 39$
Step 2 Check	Is the answer reasonable? Yes, because 39 fifth-graders are in clubs. If you round the number of students in each club, you get 35, which is close to the actual number.

2-8

Reteach

Problem-Solving Investigation (continued)

Solve each problem. If there is extra information, identify it. If there is not enough information, tell what information is needed.

1. The students in Mr. Kelly's class collected donations for a food pantry. How many more pounds of food did Patrick collect than Ryan?

Student	Pounds of Food Collected
Patrick	46
Ryan	59

_____

2. The Art Club sells 23 paintings and 19 sculptures for a total of $382. How much does a painting cost?

_____

_____

3. Complete the pattern:

5, 9, 13, 17, _____, _____, _____

4. Julie practiced shooting free throws for 200 minutes in five days. How many minutes did she practice shooting free throws each day if she practiced the same number of minutes each day?

_____

5. A pizza is cut into 12 slices. How many people can be served?

_____

_____

_____

6. Consuela earned $128 this week while working at a grocery store. She earned $45 while babysitting and $30 tutoring. How much more did she earn babysitting than tutoring?

_____

_____

_____

Name _____ Date _____

Skills Practice

Problem-Solving Investigation

Extra or Missing Information

The table shows the number of students who have volunteered to help with the production of the school play. The school has a budget of $800 to produce the play. Tickets for the play will cost $4 for adults. Students will be admitted for free. There are 500 students who attend the school.

Activity	Number of Students
Directors	3
Actors	18
Lighting	6
Sound	4
Special effects	3
Set design	8
Costume design	6
Makeup	2

If there is extra information, identify the extra information. If there is not enough information, write *not enough information*. Then tell what information you would need to solve the problem.

1. How many students who attend the school have volunteered to help with the play?

   _____

   _____

2. How many student volunteers are involved in set design and costume design?

   _____

   _____

3. If the students sell 300 tickets to the school play, will they have enough money to cover all of the expenses for the play?

   _____

   _____

Name _____ Date _____

Reteach

Selecting an Appropriate Display

Students who were putting on a production of *Oliver* had to memorize 10 songs. At the end of one week, these were the numbers of songs memorized.

Which type of graph would you use to display the data in the table?

Songs Memorized	
Number of Songs	Number of Students
1–2	18
3–4	8
5–6	0
7–8	1
9–10	1

When deciding which kind of graph to use for a set of data, consider the following:

- Is the data shown in frequency intervals?
- Do both axes have numbers?
- Are two sets of data compared?
- Does the data show a change over time?

The song data shows equal intervals. Both axes on a graph would have numbers.

A histogram is an appropriate graph for the data.

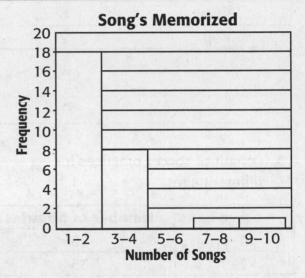

Which type of graph would you use to display the data in each problem? Explain why. Then make the graph.

1. The following test scores were recorded for a science test in Ms. Martin's class: 88, 79, 89, 92, 90, 95, 87, 89, 95, 94, 85, 83, 91, 80, and 87.

_____

_____

2. Katie kept a log of the number of sit-ups she did each day from Monday through Friday.

M	T	W	Th	F
52	75	98	80	100

_____

_____

2–9

Skills Practice

5SDAP1.2

Selecting an Appropriate Display

Which type of graph would you use to display the data in each table? Explain why.

1. CDs owned by Patrick

Type of CD	Number of CDs
Country	3
Rock	10
Rap	8
Blues	6
Pop	2

2. The number of laps completed by students jogging around Lincoln Park

Number of Laps	Number of Students
1	4
2	3
3	5
4	2

_____

4. Measurement

Time	Temperature
1 P.M.	64°F
2 P.M.	68°F
3 P.M.	70°F
4 P.M.	66°F

3. Length of soccer practices for different ages

Age	Number of Minutes
4–6	25
7–9	35
10–12	50
13–15	75

_____

Solve.

5. Write a problem in which you could use a graph to display the data. Share it with others.

_____

_____

_____

Name _____ Date _____

Reteach

Integers and Graphing

Numbers that are less than zero are called **negative numbers** and are written with a − sign. Numbers greater than zero are **positive numbers**. Negative whole numbers, zero, and positive whole numbers are **integers**.

Graph −5 and +3 on a number line.

Write an integer to represent each situation.

The temperature is 17 degrees above zero.

The word *above* means *greater than*. The integer is +17 or 17.

The diver is 3 meters below sea level.

The word *below* means *less than*. The integer is −3.

Graph each integer on a number line.

1. −2   **2.** 9   **3.** −4

4. 5   **5.** −6   **6.** 1

Write an integer to represent each situation.

7. 23 feet below sea level _____   **8.** loss of 18 pounds _____

9. profit of $74 _____   **10.** 5 degrees below zero _____

11. 14 feet above the ground _____   **12.** gain of 3 kilograms _____

13. 10 degrees above zero _____   **14.** loss of 5 ounces _____

Skills Practice

Integers and Graphing

Write an integer to represent each situation.

1. spent $15 _____

2. 11 degrees colder than 0°F _____

3. 8-yard gain in football _____

4. deposit of $25 into bank account _____

5. 10 feet below sea level _____

6. 3-centimeter increase in height _____

7. withdrawal of $50 from bank account _____

8. received $5 allowance _____

9. speed increase of 15 mph _____

10. 30 seconds before lift-off _____

Describe a situation that can be represented by the integer.

11. −17 _____

12. +$27 _____

13. +45 _____

14. −9 _____

Graph each integer on a number line.

15. +8

16. −7

17. +11

Name _____ Date _____

Reteach

Representing Decimals

The decimal 1.56 can be shown in several ways. The models below will show you different ways to represent 1.56.

You could use a place-value chart like the one below to represent 1.56.

1,000	100	10	1	0.1	0.01	0.001
Thousands	Hundreds	Tens	Ones	Tenths	Hundredths	Thousandths
0	0	0	1	5	6	

You could also represent 1.56 using a decimal model:

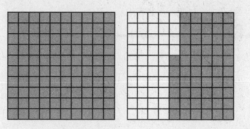

Represent the following decimals.

1. Use the place-value chart to show 0.87.

1,000	100	10	1	0.1	0.01	0.001
Thousands	Hundreds	Tens	Ones	Tenths	Hundredths	Thousandths

2. Use the decimal model to show 1.03.

Name _____ Date _____

Skills Practice

5NS1.5

Representing Decimals

Graph each decimal in the approximate position on a number line.

1. 2.8

2. 1.4

3. 5.35

Write the letter that represents each decimal on the number line below.

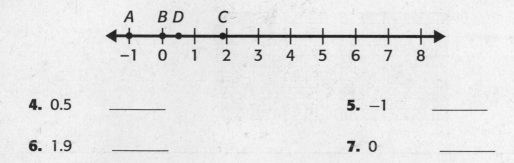

4. 0.5 _____

5. −1 _____

6. 1.9 _____

7. 0 _____

Write the decimal that represents each letter on the number line below.

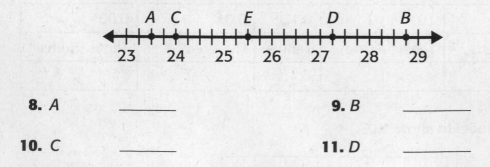

8. A _____

9. B _____

10. C _____

11. D _____

12. Lauren grew a seedling that measured 0.75 inches after 3 days. Graph this decimal on a number line.

Name _____ Date _____

Reteach

Comparing and Ordering Whole Numbers and Decimals

You can use place value to compare numbers.

- Compare 43,058 and 48,503.
  Compare the numbers, starting
  with the greatest place.

  ↓↓
  43,058
  48,503

  Since 4 = 4, compare the next place value.

  Since 3 < 8, 43,058 < 48,503.

- Compare 12.106 and 9.837.
  If the numbers have a different number
  of digits, be sure to line them up correctly.

  12.106
   9.837

  Only the number 12.106 has a digit in
  the tens place. So, 12.106 > 9.837.

Use >, < or = to compare each pair of numbers.

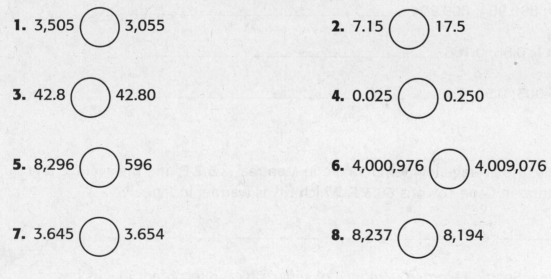

1. 3,505 ⬭ 3,055

2. 7.15 ⬭ 17.5

3. 42.8 ⬭ 42.80

4. 0.025 ⬭ 0.250

5. 8,296 ⬭ 596

6. 4,000,976 ⬭ 4,009,076

7. 3.645 ⬭ 3.654

8. 8,237 ⬭ 8,194

Name _____ Date _____

Skills Practice

Comparing and Ordering Whole Numbers and Decimals

Use >, <, or = to compare each pair of numbers.

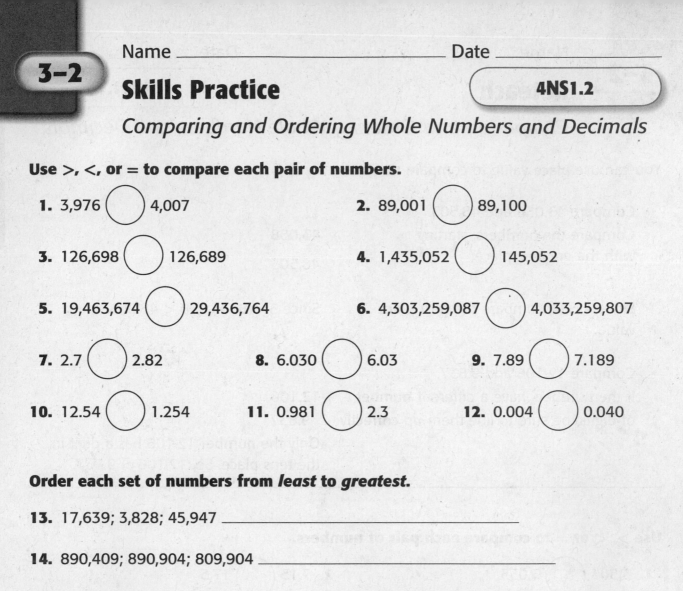

1. 3,976 ◯ 4,007

2. 89,001 ◯ 89,100

3. 126,698 ◯ 126,689

4. 1,435,052 ◯ 145,052

5. 19,463,674 ◯ 29,436,764

6. 4,303,259,087 ◯ 4,033,259,807

7. 2.7 ◯ 2.82

8. 6.030 ◯ 6.03

9. 7.89 ◯ 7.189

10. 12.54 ◯ 1.254

11. 0.981 ◯ 2.3

12. 0.004 ◯ 0.040

Order each set of numbers from *least* to *greatest*.

13. 17,639; 3,828; 45,947 _____

14. 890,409; 890,904; 809,904 _____

15. 0.186; 0.1; 0.86; 0.168 _____

16. 5.309; 5.003; 0.53; 0.9 _____

Solve.

17. In January, the average low temperature in Montreal is 5.2°F, and the average low temperature in Cape Town is 60.3°F. Which city is warmer in January?

_____

18. In one year Seattle recorded 0.24 inch of snow, Chicago recorded 30.9 inches of snow, and Birmingham recorded 1 inch of snow. Write these amounts in order from least to greatest.

_____

Name _____ Date _____

Reteach

Rounding Whole Numbers and Decimals

Rounding Whole Numbers and Decimals

You can round whole numbers and decimals the same way:

Step 1

Underline the digit of the place value being rounded.

Step 2

Look at the digit to its right. If it is 4 or less, the underlined digit stays the same. If it is 5 or greater, add 1 to the underlined digit.

Step 3

After rounding, replace the remaining digits to the right with zeros.

Round 2,876,301 to the nearest million.

Step 1: Underline the digit to be rounded: _____

Step 2: Look at the digit to its right. Is it 4 or less or 5 or greater? _____

Step 3: The rounded number is: _____

Round 67.01 to the nearest tenth.

Step 1: Underline the digit to be rounded: _____

Step 2: Look at the digit to its right. Is it 4 or less or 5 or greater? _____

Step 3: The rounded number is: _____

Round each whole number to the indicated place-value position.

1. 4,583,304; thousand _____

2. 62,893,665; million _____

3. 12,887,329; ten million _____

4. 7,623,873; ten thousand _____

Round each decimal to the indicated place-value position.

5. 90.763; ones _____

6. 0.337; hundredths _____

7. 42.7456; thousandths _____

8. 55.23; tens _____

3-3

Skills Practice

5NS1.1

Rounding Whole Numbers and Decimals

Round each decimal to the indicated place-value position.

1. 0.463; tenths _____

2. 32.877; hundredths _____

3. 5.65689; thousandths _____

4. 3.48; ones _____

5. 56.45; tens _____

6. 4.67; hundredths _____

7. 13.8908; tenths _____

8. 21.9; tens _____

9. The price of a gallon of milk is $3.75. How much is this to the nearest dollar?

_____

Round each whole number to the indicated place-value position.

10. 3,579; thousand _____

11. 29,342; hundred _____

12. 433,231,292; million _____

13. 711,900; hundred thousand _____

14. 33,110; ten thousand _____

15. 132,509; ten _____

16. 559,308; ten thousand _____

17. 14,663; hundred _____

18. 8,413; thousand _____

19. There are about 77,621,001 pet cats in the United States. How many pet cats are there rounded to the nearest hundred thousand?

_____

3-4

Reteach

Problem-Solving Strategy

Use Logical Reasoning

Of a group of people surveyed, 28 said they go to baseball games and 14 said they go to hockey games. Seven of the people said they go to both. How many people said they go to hockey games but not baseball games?

Step 1 Understand	**What facts do you know?** • Of those surveyed, _____ go to baseball games, _____ go to hockey games, and _____ go to both types of games. **What do you need to find?** • The number of people _____ _____
Step 2 Plan • Logical reasoning • Draw a picture or diagram • Make a graph • Act it out • Make a table or list • Find a pattern • Guess and check • Write an equation • Work backward • Solve a simpler problem	**Make a plan.** Choose a strategy. You can draw a Venn diagram to solve the problem. One circle shows the number of people who go to baseball games. The other circle shows the number of people who go to hockey games. The overlapping part of the circles shows the number of people who go to both. Number who go to baseball games Both Number who go to hockey games

3-4

Reteach

5MR2.4, 5MG1.4

Problem-Solving Strategy   *(continued)*

Step 3 Solve	**Carry out your plan.** How many people go to both types of games? Write the number in the overlapping section of the Venn diagram.

The two sections of the circle for hockey must add up to 14. You can use logical reasoning to find the number of people who only go to hockey games.

Use the Venn diagram. So, _____ + _____ = _____

How many people go to hockey games, but not

baseball games? _____

| Step 4 Check | **Is the solution reasonable?** Look back at the problem. Have you answered the question? _____

How can you check your answer?

_____ |
|---|---|

Solve.

1. Of 25 pet owners surveyed, 16 have a dog and 12 have a cat. Three people have both a cat and a dog. How many of the pet owners have only dogs?

   _____

Name _____ Date _____

Skills Practice

Problem-Solving Strategy

Use the *logical reasoning* strategy to solve.

1. Of 26 people surveyed, 19 said they go to basketball games and 12 said they go to football games. Five of the people said they go to both. How many people said they go to basketball games, but not to football games?

   _____

2. **Music** Of 40 teachers surveyed, 34 said they listen to classical music and 17 said they listen to opera. Eleven of the teachers said they listen to both classical music and opera. How many teachers listen to classical music, but not to opera?

   _____

3. Of 24 students surveyed, 17 students said they liked board games and 12 said they like card games. Five students said they liked both. How many students said they like board games, but not card games?

   _____

4. **Health** Of the 50 people surveyed at a recreation center, 32 said they used the basketball courts and 24 said they used the racquetball courts. Six of the people said they used both courts. How many people said they use the racquetball courts, but not the basketball courts?

   _____

5. Nathan wants to buy trading cards. Superstar packages cost $3.23 each and mixed packages cost $1.78 each. Nathan buys 7 packages and spends a total of $15.36. How many of each type of package did he buy?

   _____

6. Write a problem that you could use logical reasoning to solve. Share it with a classmate.

   _____

Name _____ Date _____

Reteach

Estimating Sums and Differences

To estimate a sum or difference, you can round the numbers first. This can make it easier to add or subtract mentally.

Method 1: Use front-end estimation.

$$
\begin{array}{r}
①8.7 \rightarrow 10 \\
-④.2 \rightarrow -4 \\
\hline
6
\end{array}
$$

Circle the digit in the greatest place. Add or subtract.

Method 2: Use rounding to estimate.

$$
\begin{array}{r}
18.7 \rightarrow 19 \\
-4.2 \rightarrow -4 \\
\hline
15
\end{array}
$$

Find the lesser number. Circle the digit in the greatest place. Round each number to that place. Add or subtract.

Round using front-end estimation to find each sum or difference.

1. $\begin{array}{r} 4.204 \rightarrow \\ +\ 2.779 \rightarrow \\ \hline \end{array}$

2. $\begin{array}{r} \$189 \rightarrow \\ -\ 53 \rightarrow \\ \hline \end{array}$

3. $\begin{array}{r} 4.567 \rightarrow \\ -\ 1.788 \rightarrow \\ \hline \end{array}$

4. $\begin{array}{r} 31.53 \rightarrow \\ +\ 42.07 \rightarrow \\ \hline \end{array}$

5. $\begin{array}{r} 15.497 \rightarrow \\ +\ 8.38 \rightarrow \\ \hline \end{array}$

6. $\begin{array}{r} 47.1 \ \rightarrow \\ -11.66 \rightarrow \\ \hline \end{array}$

Estimate each sum or difference using rounding.

7. $\begin{array}{r} 5.087 \rightarrow \\ +\ 9.615 \rightarrow \\ \hline \end{array}$

8. $\begin{array}{r} 794 \rightarrow \\ +\ 3,157 \rightarrow \\ \hline \end{array}$

9. $\begin{array}{r} 4,780 \rightarrow \\ -\ 103 \rightarrow \\ \hline \end{array}$

10. $\begin{array}{r} \$42.469 \rightarrow \\ +\ 8.23 \ \rightarrow \\ \hline \end{array}$

11. $\begin{array}{r} 58.9 \rightarrow \\ -\ 7.1 \rightarrow \\ \hline \end{array}$

12. $\begin{array}{r} 32.78 \rightarrow \\ -\ 6.6 \ \rightarrow \\ \hline \end{array}$

Name _____ Date _____

Skills Practice

Estimating Sums and Differences

Estimate using rounding.

1. 68.99 + 22.31 _____

2. 39.57 + 18.34 _____

3. 81.25 − 23.16 _____

4. 21.56 − 19.62 _____

5. 5.69 + 3.47 + 8.02 _____

6. 6.6 + 1.22 + 5.54 _____

Estimate using clustering.

7. $4.56 + $4.79 + $5.21 + $5.38

_____

8. 9.7325 + 9.55 + 10.333

_____

9. 39.8 + 39.6 + 40.21 + 40.47

_____

10. $69.72 + $70.44 + $70.59 + $69.56

_____

Estimate using front-end estimation.

11. 34.87 − 29.12 _____

12. 69.45 − 44.8 _____

13. $78.69 + $31.49 _____

14. $258.32 + $378.60 _____

Solve.

15. SHOPPING Miriam bought a basketball for $24.99 and basketball shoes for $47.79. About how much did Miriam spend on the ball and shoes? _____

16. PRECIPITATION Albuquerque gets an average of 6.35 inches of precipitation a year. Phoenix gets an average of 6.82 inches a year. About how many more inches of precipitation does Phoenix get than Albuquerque using rounding and using front-end estimation?

_____

60

Name _____ Date _____

Reteach

Problem-Solving Investigation

5MR2.6, 5NS1.1

Chapter Resources

Use Estimation

One strategy in solving problems is to estimate. Here is an example of a problem that asks you to use estimating to solve.

The Fernandez family is keeping a chart of how much weight their new puppy gains each week. Look at the chart and estimate how much total weight the puppy has gained in the first 6 weeks.

Week	Weight gained (pounds)
1	1.09
2	1.3
3	0.3
4	2.03
5	0.75
6	1.90

Step 1 Understand	**What facts do you know?** You know the actual amounts of weight gained by the puppy each week for the first 6 weeks. **What do you need to find?** You need to estimate the amount of weight the puppy has gained in the first 6 weeks.
Plan	You do not need an exact answer, so you can estimate the number of pounds the puppy has gained in the first 6 weeks. Round the decimals to whole numbers, and then add.
Solve	Week 1 $\longrightarrow$ 1.09 $\longrightarrow$ 1 Week 2 $\longrightarrow$ 1.3 $\longrightarrow$ 1 Week 3 $\longrightarrow$ 0.3 $\longrightarrow$ 0 Week 4 $\longrightarrow$ 2.03 $\longrightarrow$ 2 Week 5 $\longrightarrow$ 0.75 $\longrightarrow$ 1 Week 6 $\longrightarrow$ 1.90 $\longrightarrow$ $\underline{2}$ $\qquad\qquad\qquad\qquad\qquad\qquad$ 7 The puppy has gained about 7 pounds in the first 6 weeks.
Check	Use clustering. Since $1 \times 7 = 7$, 7 is a reasonable answer.

3-6

Reteach

5MR2.6, 5NS1.1

Problem-Solving Investigation (continued)

Answer the questions and solve.

1. Molly earned the following amounts in her job last week: $12.22, 9.05, and 13.56. About how much did Molly earn?

   What do you know?

   _____

   _____

   What is your plan?

   _____

   Solve. _____

2. Jorges volunteers at the Senior Center on weekends. During the last 4 weekends, he has volunteered for 2.5 hours, 1.7 hours, 3.1 hours, and 1.5 hours. For about how long has Jorges volunteered in the last 4 weekends?

   What do you know?

   _____

   _____

   What is your plan?

   _____

   Solve. _____

Name _____ **Date** _____

Skills Practice

Problem-Solving Investigation

Solve. Did you give an estimate or exact answer? Explain.

1. It costs Matt a little more than $4 a day to feed his dog. How much does it cost him to feed his dog for a year?

   _____

2. In the past year, a grocery store deposited about 6 million pennies, 3 million nickels, 4 million dimes, and 2 million quarters in the bank. What is the total value of the deposit?

   _____

3. A bank puts 3,000 quarters in each bag. How much are 15 bags of quarters worth?

   _____

4. A vault contains $3,000 worth of nickels. How many nickels are in the vault?

   _____

5. When at rest, your heart probably beats about 70 times per minute. At that rate, how many times does it beat in an hour?

   _____

6. Ann bought two shirts for $28.95 each and a skirt for $33.95. The sales tax was $3.71. How much did she pay altogether?

   _____

Choose the correct answer.

It costs $0.38 to produce and mail a newsletter. Each week, 475,000 newsletters are mailed to subscribers.

7. Which of the following statements is true?

   A The cost of producing and sending newsletters for one month is about $2,000,000.

   B More than 12,000,000 newsletters are produced and mailed in a three-month period.

   C The cost for two months is about $1,444,000.

   D About 160,000 newsletters are produced and mailed each month.

8. If the numbers in a problem appear to be rounded, you can

   F find an exact answer.

   G estimate the answer.

   H ignore the numbers in the problem.

   J check your answer.

Name _____ Date _____

Reteach

Greatest Common Factor

The GCF (greatest common factor) of two numbers is the greatest number that is a factor of both.

Find the GCF of 12 and 16.
Factors of 12: 1, 2, 3, 4, 6, 12
Factors of 16: 1, 2, 4, 8, 16
The GCF of 12 and 16 is 4.

Find the GCF of 20 and 24.
Factors of 20: 1, 2, 4, 5, 10, 20
Factors of 24: 1, 2, 3, 4, 6, 8, 12, and 24
The GCF of 20 and 24 is 4.

List all the factors of each number. Circle each set of common factors. Then identify the GCF.

1. 8: _____, _____, _____, _____

32: _____, _____, _____, _____, _____, _____

GCF: _____

2. 9: _____, _____, _____

15: _____, _____, _____, _____

GCF: _____

3. 6: _____, _____, _____, _____

42: _____, _____, _____, _____, _____, _____,

_____, _____

GCF: _____

Find the greatest common factor (GCF) of each set of numbers.

4. 28 and 40 _____   **5.** 10 and 25 _____   **6.** 18 and 24 _____

7. 14 and 21 _____   **8.** 35 and 42 _____   **9.** 15, 25, 30 _____

Grade 5

Chapter 4

Name _____ Date _____

Skills Practice

6NS2.4

Greatest Common Factor

Identify the common factors of each set of numbers.

1. 36, 40 _____

2. 55, 77 _____

3. 8, 20, 36 _____

4. 15, 30, 40 _____

Find the GCF of each set of numbers.

5. 10 and 15 _____

6. 6 and 24 _____

7. 16 and 36 _____

8. 24 and 30 _____

9. 9 and 21 _____

10. 12 and 40 _____

11. 8 and 28 _____

12. 18 and 27 _____

13. 12 and 60 _____

14. 14 and 18 _____

15. 20 and 30 _____

16. 24 and 45 _____

17. 27 and 30 _____

18. 10 and 22 _____

19. 12 and 36 _____

20. 11 and 15 _____

21. 4, 12, and 30 _____

22. 12, 18, and 36 _____

23. 9, 16, and 25 _____

24. 9, 15, and 21 _____

25. 12, 15, and 21 _____

26. 9, 36, and 45 _____

Solve.

27. Thirty people at the nature center signed up for hiking, and 18 signed up for bird watching. They will be divided up into smaller groups. What is the greatest number of people that can be in each group and have all groups the same size?

_____

28. Rosa found 8 different wildflowers and 20 different leaves on her hike. She plans to display them in 7 equal rows on a poster. What is the greatest number of flowers or leaves she can put in each row?

_____

Name _____ Date _____

Reteach

Problem-Solving Strategy

Make an Organized List

Otto plays a game. He spins two spinners and finds the sum of the numbers he lands on. What sums can Otto make?

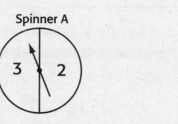

Spinner A

Spinner B

Step 1 Understand	**What do you know?** Spinner A is marked _____ and Spinner B is marked _____. **What do you need to find?** What _____ Otto can make.
Step 2 Plan	**Make a plan.** You can make an organized list to solve the problem. *Remember:* A sum is the answer to an addition problem.
Step 3 Solve	**Carry out your plan** Make a list of possible sums.

Spinner A		Spinner B	Sum
+			=
+			=
+			=
+			=

Name _____   Date _____

Reteach

Problem-Solving Strategy (continued)

Step 3 Solve	
	$\underline{\hspace{2cm}} + \underline{\hspace{2cm}} = \underline{\hspace{2cm}}$ $\underline{\hspace{2cm}} + \underline{\hspace{2cm}} = \underline{\hspace{2cm}}$ What sums can Otto make? _____
Step 4 Check	**Is the solution reasonable?** Reread the problem. Have you answered the question? How can you check your answer? _____ _____ _____

Solve using the *make an organized list* strategy.

1. A spinner has 3 equal sections that are white, yellow, and green. Another spinner has 3 equal sections that are blue, purple, and red. How many different combinations of colors are possible if you spin each spinner once?

   _____

2. Liz has 4 different rings and 3 different bracelets. If she wears one ring and one bracelet, how many different combinations can she make?

   _____

4–2

Skills Practice

Problem-Solving Strategy

5MR.1.1, 5NS1.4

Make an organized list.

Solve. Use the *make an organized list* strategy.

1. Tom has a blue shirt, a red shirt, and a yellow shirt. He also has a pair of blue jeans, a pair of khaki pants, and a pair of corduroys. How many combinations of shirt and pants are possible?

   _____

2. If you have ham, turkey, and roast beef, with wheat, white, and rye bread along with mayonnaise and mustard, how many sandwich combinations are possible? Hint: Choose only one meat, one bread, and one condiment.

   _____

3. Allie has square beads that are red, blue, and green. She has round beads that are yellow and white. If she chooses one color from each shape of beads, how many combinations of colors can she have?

   _____

4. **Health** Ms. Dawson eats a fruit and a vegetable for lunch each day. She selects an apple, a banana, an orange, or a pear for her fruit. She chooses carrot sticks, celery sticks, or green-pepper slices for her vegetable. How many combinations of 1 fruit and 1 vegetable can she make?

   _____

Solve. Use any strategy.

5. There are three girls, Jackie, Janey, and Janelle. How many different ways can the girls be lined up?

   _____

6. Greta orders stickers that come with 12 sheets per package. Each sheet has 10 rows of stickers and each row has 8 stickers. How many stickers are in each package?

   _____

4-3

Reteach

5NS2.3

Simplifying Fractions

When a fraction is in simplest form, 1 is the only common factor of its numerator and denominator.

Write in simplest form: $\frac{16}{40}$

Step 1
Find the GCF of the numerator and the denominator.

Factors of 16: 1, 2, 4, **8**, 16
Factors of 40: 1, 2, 4, 5, **8**, 10, 20, 40
GCF: 8

Step 2
Divide the numerator and the denominator by their GCF.

$$\frac{16}{40} = \frac{16 \div 8}{40 \div 8} = \frac{2}{5}$$

Check that $\frac{2}{5}$ is in simplest form.

Factors of 2: 1, 2
Factors of 5: 1, 5

The only common factor of 2 and 5 is 1, so $\frac{2}{5}$ is in simplest form.

Write each fraction in simplest form.

1. $\frac{6}{10}$

Factors of 6: _____

Factors of 10: _____

Simplest Form:

_____

2. $\frac{9}{36}$

Factors of 9: _____

Factors of 36: _____

Simplest Form:

_____

3. $\frac{12}{30}$

Factors of 12: _____

Factors of 30: _____

Simplest Form:

_____

4. $\frac{20}{25}$

Factors of 20: _____

Factors of 25: _____

Simplest Form:

_____

5. $\frac{6}{18}$ _____

6. $\frac{15}{40}$ _____

7. $\frac{8}{30}$ _____

8. $\frac{24}{27}$ _____

9. $\frac{16}{28}$ _____

10. $\frac{30}{48}$ _____

11. $\frac{20}{24}$ _____

12. $\frac{21}{28}$ _____

Name _Eric_ Date _____

Skills Practice

Simplifying Fractions

Replace each *x* with a number so the fractions are equivalent.

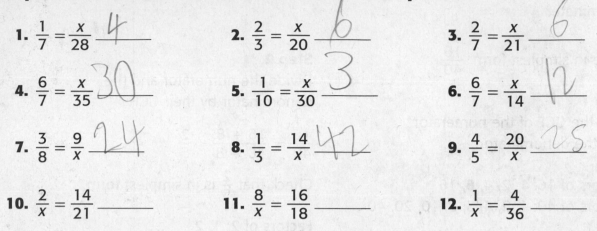

1. $\dfrac{1}{7} = \dfrac{x}{28}$ _4_

2. $\dfrac{2}{3} = \dfrac{x}{20}$ _6_

3. $\dfrac{2}{7} = \dfrac{x}{21}$ _6_

4. $\dfrac{6}{7} = \dfrac{x}{35}$ _30_

5. $\dfrac{1}{10} = \dfrac{x}{30}$ _3_

6. $\dfrac{6}{7} = \dfrac{x}{14}$ _12_

7. $\dfrac{3}{8} = \dfrac{9}{x}$ _24_

8. $\dfrac{1}{3} = \dfrac{14}{x}$ _42_

9. $\dfrac{4}{5} = \dfrac{20}{x}$ _25_

10. $\dfrac{2}{x} = \dfrac{14}{21}$ _____

11. $\dfrac{8}{x} = \dfrac{16}{18}$ _____

12. $\dfrac{1}{x} = \dfrac{4}{36}$ _____

Write each fraction in simplest form. If the fraction is already in simplest form, write *simplest form*.

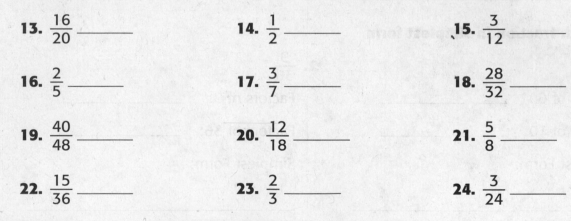

13. $\dfrac{16}{20}$ _____

14. $\dfrac{1}{2}$ _____

15. $\dfrac{3}{12}$ _____

16. $\dfrac{2}{5}$ _____

17. $\dfrac{3}{7}$ _____

18. $\dfrac{28}{32}$ _____

19. $\dfrac{40}{48}$ _____

20. $\dfrac{12}{18}$ _____

21. $\dfrac{5}{8}$ _____

22. $\dfrac{15}{36}$ _____

23. $\dfrac{2}{3}$ _____

24. $\dfrac{3}{24}$ _____

Solve.

25. Of the 27 students in Jarrod's class, 18 receive an allowance each week. What fraction of the students, in simplest form, receive an allowance?

_____

26. Of the 18 students who receive an allowance, 14 do chores around the house. What fraction of these students, in simplest form, do chores around the house?

_____

Name _____ Date _____

Reteach

Mixed Numbers and Improper Fractions

Chapter Resources

A **mixed number** is made up of a whole number and a fraction. An **improper fraction** is a fraction in which the numerator is greater than or equal to the denominator.

Write $2\frac{2}{3}$ as an improper fraction.

Step 1	**Step 2**	**Step 3**
Multiply the whole number by the denominator.	Add the numerator to the product.	Write the sum over the denominator.
$2\frac{2}{3} \longrightarrow 2 \times 3 = 6$	$6 + 2 = 8$	$2\frac{2}{3} = \frac{8}{3}$

Write $\frac{13}{4}$ as a mixed number.

Step 1	**Step 2**	**Step 3**
Divide the numerator by the denominator.	Write the quotient as the whole-number part of the mixed number.	Write the remainder as the numerator of the fraction.
$\frac{13}{4} \longrightarrow \begin{array}{r} 3 \\ 4\overline{)13} \\ \underline{12} \\ 1 \end{array}$	$\frac{13}{4} \longrightarrow 3\frac{1}{4}$	$\frac{13}{4} = 3\frac{1}{4}$

Write each mixed number as an improper fraction.

1. $2\frac{2}{7}$ _____

2. $5\frac{3}{4}$ _____

3. $6\frac{5}{8}$ _____

Write each improper fraction as a mixed number.

4. $\frac{9}{8}$ _____

5. $\frac{7}{2}$ _____

6. $\frac{12}{5}$ _____

4-4

Skills Practice

Mixed Numbers and Improper Fractions

Write each mixed number as an improper fraction.

1. $2\frac{3}{4}$ _____

2. $5\frac{1}{6}$ _____

3. $8\frac{1}{2}$ _____

4. $3\frac{2}{3}$ _____

5. $7\frac{2}{5}$ _____

6. $1\frac{9}{10}$ _____

7. $4\frac{7}{8}$ _____

8. $6\frac{5}{7}$ _____

9. $1\frac{8}{9}$ _____

10. $3\frac{12}{17}$ _____

11. $2\frac{1}{10}$ _____

12. $5\frac{5}{13}$ _____

13. $2\frac{2}{7}$ _____

14. $5\frac{3}{4}$ _____

15. $6\frac{5}{8}$ _____

16. $3\frac{4}{10}$ _____

17. $9\frac{1}{3}$ _____

18. $4\frac{4}{5}$ _____

19. $9\frac{1}{2}$ _____

20. $4\frac{6}{9}$ _____

Write each improper fraction as a mixed number or a whole number.

21. $\frac{18}{12}$ _____

22. $\frac{22}{3}$ _____

23. $\frac{27}{9}$ _____

24. $\frac{14}{4}$ _____

25. $\frac{28}{6}$ _____

26. $\frac{64}{8}$ _____

27. $\frac{13}{5}$ _____

28. $\frac{46}{8}$ _____

29. $\frac{21}{8}$ _____

30. $\frac{64}{35}$ _____

31. $\frac{19}{3}$ _____

32. $\frac{44}{8}$ _____

33. $\frac{10}{9}$ _____

34. $\frac{3}{1}$ _____

35. $\frac{4}{3}$ _____

36. $\frac{6}{5}$ _____

37. $\frac{7}{6}$ _____

38. $\frac{18}{4}$ _____

39. $\frac{20}{11}$ _____

40. $\frac{3}{2}$ _____

Solve.

41. A shipment of boxes weighs 30 pounds. There are 8 boxes and each weighs the same number of pounds. How much does each box weigh?

42. Each box in another shipment weighs $3\frac{1}{6}$ pounds. There are 6 boxes in the shipment. What is the total weight of the shipment?

_____

_____

Name _____ Date _____

Reteach

Least Common Multiple

Find the **least common multiple** (LCM) of 12 and 18.
List the multiples of each number.

Multiples of 12: 12, 24, **36**, 48, 60, 72, 84,...
Multiples of 18: 18, **36**, 54,...

Name the least common multiple (LCM): 36

List the multiples of each number. Then find the least common multiple (LCM) of each set of numbers.

1. 10 and 15 _____

_____

2. 14 and 21 _____

_____

_____

3. 12 and 13 _____

_____

_____

4. 15 and 25 _____

_____

_____

5. 15 and 18 _____

_____

6. 9 and 21 _____

_____

Find the least common multiple (LCM) of each set of numbers.

7. 2 and 12 _____

8. 4 and 9 _____

9. 6 and 10 _____

10. 3 and 5 _____

11. 12 and 15 _____

12. 12 and 20 _____

13. 3, 6, and 8 _____

14. 5, 6, and 10 _____

4-5

Skills Practice

Least Common Multiple

Identify the first three common multiples of each set of numbers.

1. 2, 5 _____

2. 1, 6 _____

3. 2, 3, 4 _____

4. 7, 14 _____

Find the least common multiple (LCM) of the numbers.

5. 5 and 15 _____   6. 2 and 9 _____   7. 2 and 11 _____

8. 6 and 9 _____   9. 4 and 5 _____   10. 8 and 12 _____

11. 4 and 8 _____   12. 10 and 25 _____   13. 3 and 4 _____

14. 2 and 3 _____   15. 8 and 9 _____   16. 4 and 10 _____

17. 2, 4, and 16 _____   18. 3, 5, and 6 _____   19. 3, 6, and 8 _____

Solve.

20. José and Sara are walking around the track at the same time. José walks one lap every 8 minutes. Sara walks a lap every 6 minutes. What is the least amount of time they would both have to walk for them to cross the starting point together?

_____

21. Pamela and David walk on the same track. It takes Pamela 9 minutes and David 6 minutes to walk one lap. If they start walking at the same time, how many laps will each have walked when they cross the starting point together for the first time?

_____

4–6

Reteach

5MR2.6, 5SDAP1.2

Problem-Solving Investigation

Choose the Best Strategy

Saturday, the Stevensons went shopping and spent a total of $40 on meat for dinners for the week. They purchased chicken for $3 per pound and some hamburger for $2 per pound. They spent three times as much money on chicken as on hamburger. How many pounds of chicken and how many pounds of hamburger did the family purchase?

Step 1 Understand	**What do you know?** You know the Stevensons spent $40 on meat. You know chicken costs $3 per pound and hamburger costs $2 per pound. You also know the family spent three times as much on chicken as on hamburger. **What do you need to find?** How many pounds of chicken and hamburger the family purchased.
Step 2 Plan	Choose a strategy. Will it help to make a table, list, or number line so you can see how numbers change? You may need to guess and check a few times to find the information that you need. A table would help you compare the amount spent on chicken to the amount spent on hamburger.
Step 3 Solve	Use a ____ for the number that's missing. $3 × ____ + $2 × ____ = $40. ($3 × ____) + ($2 × ____) = $40
Step 4 Check	($3 × 10) + ($2 × 5) = $40 $30 + $10 = $40

4-6

Reteach

Problem-Solving Investigation   (continued)

Use any strategy shown below to solve.

- Guess and check.   • Make an organized list.
- Make a table.

1. Marcie wants to sit by her three sisters at the school assembly. How many different ways can they sit together along one row?

_____

2. A department store has the following options for jackets:

Jacket	Color
rain slicker	blue
windbreaker	black
spring jacket	green
jean jacket	

How many combinations of style and color are possible?

_____

3. Jennifer is taking a trip around the country. She wants to go to Oregon, Washington, and New Mexico. How many different ways can Jennifer take her trip?

_____

4. Selena is making a pizza for dinner. She has mushrooms, onions, and pineapple to put on the pizza. How many different pizzas can Selena make with toppings?

_____

5. Jenna is planning a birthday party for her brother. She needs to buy a gift, decorate the house, and make some punch. How many different ways can Jenna complete all of the tasks?

_____

4–6

Skills Practice

Problem-Solving Investigation

5MR2.6, 5SDAP1.2

Choose any strategy shown below to solve.

- • Guess and check.
- • Make an organized list.
- • Make a table.

1. The school basketball team scored enough points to win. They scored 1 point every 5 minutes. How many points did they score in 20 minutes?

_____

2. Forty players tried out for the team. Half of them gave up after the first set of challenges. One-fourth of the remaining players lacked skills and quit. How many players were left?

_____

3. Jerry made 42 baskets during the first season that he played. His team played 12 games. If he played in 2 games out of every 4 that the team played and he made an equal number of baskets each of these games, how many baskets did he make each game?

_____

4. Patty's goal was to make 40 baskets. She made 5 baskets in the first game she played, 5 baskets in the second game, and 10 baskets in the third game. What fraction of her goal did she make?

_____

5. The coach gave each player points after each game for being a good sport. At the end of the season, the player with the most points gets a basketball to keep. Davina scored one point in the first game and one more each game than she had in the previous game for 5 games. Sally got 3 points each game for 4 games. Who had the most points?

_____

4–7

Reteach

5SDAP1.3

Comparing Fractions

To compare fractions, rewrite them with a common denominator. Then compare the numerators.

Compare: $\frac{4}{9}$, $\frac{5}{6}$

Step 1

Find the LCD of 9 and 6.

Multiples of 9: 9, 18, 27, 36
Multiples of 6: 6, 12, 18
LCD: 18

Step 2

Write equivalent fractions.

$$\frac{4}{9} = \frac{4 \times 2}{9 \times 2} = \frac{8}{18}$$

$$\frac{5}{6} = \frac{5 \times 3}{6 \times 3} = \frac{15}{18}$$

Step 3

Compare the numerators.

$8 < 15$

Since $8 < 15$,

then $\frac{4}{9} < \frac{5}{6}$.

Replace each ● with <, >, or = to make a true sentence.

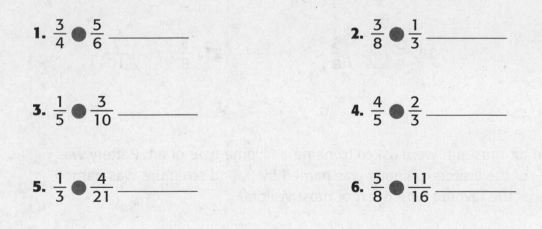

1. $\frac{3}{4}$ ● $\frac{5}{6}$ _____

2. $\frac{3}{8}$ ● $\frac{1}{3}$ _____

3. $\frac{1}{5}$ ● $\frac{3}{10}$ _____

4. $\frac{4}{5}$ ● $\frac{2}{3}$ _____

5. $\frac{1}{3}$ ● $\frac{4}{21}$ _____

6. $\frac{5}{8}$ ● $\frac{11}{16}$ _____

Name _____ Date _____

Skills Practice

Comparing Fractions

Replace each ◯ with <, >, or = to make a true sentence.

1. $\dfrac{3}{4}$ ◯ $\dfrac{7}{12}$

2. $\dfrac{2}{5}$ ◯ $\dfrac{3}{4}$

3. $\dfrac{1}{6}$ ◯ $\dfrac{1}{3}$

4. $\dfrac{1}{2}$ ◯ $\dfrac{7}{10}$

5. $\dfrac{15}{16}$ ◯ $\dfrac{3}{8}$

6. $\dfrac{3}{8}$ ◯ $\dfrac{5}{6}$

7. $\dfrac{7}{8}$ ◯ $\dfrac{8}{9}$

8. $\dfrac{2}{10}$ ◯ $\dfrac{1}{5}$

9. $\dfrac{11}{12}$ ◯ $\dfrac{5}{8}$

10. $\dfrac{4}{5}$ ◯ $\dfrac{17}{20}$

11. $\dfrac{1}{8}$ ◯ $\dfrac{2}{5}$

12. $\dfrac{2}{3}$ ◯ $\dfrac{4}{6}$

13. $\dfrac{1}{5}$ ◯ $\dfrac{1}{4}$

14. $\dfrac{5}{8}$ ◯ $\dfrac{3}{5}$

15. $\dfrac{1}{6}$ ◯ $\dfrac{4}{18}$

16. $\dfrac{2}{5}$ ◯ $\dfrac{3}{20}$

17. $\dfrac{1}{3}$ ◯ $\dfrac{1}{9}$

18. $\dfrac{3}{8}$ ◯ $\dfrac{3}{4}$

19. $\dfrac{7}{8}$ ◯ $\dfrac{4}{5}$

20. $\dfrac{5}{9}$ ◯ $\dfrac{5}{8}$

21. $\dfrac{5}{8}$ ◯ $\dfrac{7}{10}$

Solve.

22. Visitors to an art museum were asked to name a favorite type of art. Pottery was named by $\dfrac{9}{40}$ of the visitors, painting was named by $\dfrac{2}{5}$, and sculpture was named by $\dfrac{3}{8}$. What was the favorite type of art of most visitors?

_____

Name _____ Date _____

Reteach

Writing Decimals as Fractions

You can write a decimal as a fraction. Think of place value. Then simplify the fraction if necessary.

Write 0.12 as a fraction.   Think: 12 hundredths

Write: $\dfrac{12}{100}$

Simplify: $\dfrac{12}{100} = \dfrac{12 \div 4}{100 \div 4} = \dfrac{3}{25}$ So, $0.12 = \dfrac{3}{25}$.

Write 0.25 as a fraction.   Think: 25 hundredths

Write: $\dfrac{25}{100} = \dfrac{25 \div 25}{100 \div 25} = \dfrac{1}{4}$

Write each decimal as a fraction in simplest form.

1. 0.65

Think: 65 _____

Write: $\dfrac{65}{}$

Simplify: $\dfrac{65}{} = \dfrac{65 \div}{ \div} =$

2. 0.6

Think: _____

Write:

Simplify: $\dfrac{}{} = \dfrac{6 \div}{ \div} =$

3. 0.86 _____   **4.** 0.57 _____   **5.** 0.5 _____   **6.** 0.68 _____

7. 0.25 _____   **8.** 0.15 _____   **9.** 0.40 _____   **10.** 0.9 _____

11. 0.33 _____   **12.** 0.10 _____   **13.** 0.75 _____   **14.** 0.98 _____

15. 0.20 _____   **16.** 0.50 _____   **17.** 0.12 _____   **18.** 0.78 _____

19. 0.4 _____   **20.** 0.70 _____   **21.** 0.05 _____   **22.** 0.67 _____

23. 0.3 _____   **24.** 0.11 _____

4-8

Skills Practice

Writing Decimals as Fractions

Write each decimal as a fraction in simplest form.

1. 0.3 _____   **2.** 0.49 _____   **3.** 0.7 _____   **4.** 0.50 _____

5. 0.94 _____   **6.** 0.80 _____   **7.** 0.72 _____   **8.** 0.2 _____

9. 0.55 _____   **10.** 0.1 _____   **11.** 0.25 _____   **12.** 0.03 _____

13. 0.77 _____   **14.** 0.6 _____   **15.** 0.26 _____   **16.** 0.99 _____

17. 0.36 _____   **18.** 0.75 _____   **19.** 0.70 _____   **20.** 0.4 _____

Write each decimal as a mixed number in simplest form.

21. 8.9 _____   **22.** 12.1 _____   **23.** 14.5 _____   **24.** 17.03 _____

25. 9.35 _____   **26.** 42.96 _____   **27.** 7.425 _____   **28.** 50.60 _____

29. 8.43 _____   **30.** 3.25 _____   **31.** 2.25 _____   **32.** 1.33 _____

33. 4.10 _____   **34.** 7.75 _____   **35.** 8.60 _____   **36.** 16.03 _____

Solve.

37. The largest butterfly in the world is found in Papua, New Guinea. The female of the species weighs about 0.9 ounce. Use a fraction to write the female's weight.

_____

38. The shortest recorded fish is the dwarf goby found in the Indo-Pacific. The female of this species is about thirty-five hundredths inch long. Use the decimal to write the female's length.

_____

Name _____ Date _____

Reteach

5MR2.5, 5NS1.1

Rounding Fractions and Mixed Numbers

Round Up

If the numerator is almost as large as the denominator, round the number up to the next whole number.

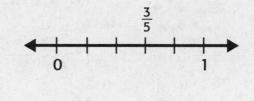

Example: $\frac{9}{10}$ rounds to 1.

9 is almost as large as 10.

Round to $\frac{1}{2}$

If the numerator is about half of the denominator, round the fraction to $\frac{1}{2}$.

Example: $\frac{3}{5}$ rounds to $\frac{1}{2}$.

3 is about half of 5.

Round Down

If the numerator is much smaller than the denominator, round the number down to the previous whole number.

Example: $\frac{1}{5}$ rounds to 0.

1 is much smaller than 5.

Round each number to the nearest half.

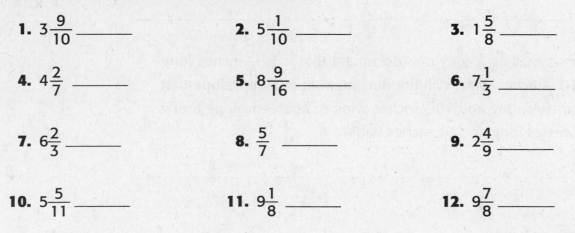

1. $3\frac{9}{10}$ _____   2. $5\frac{1}{10}$ _____   3. $1\frac{5}{8}$ _____

4. $4\frac{2}{7}$ _____   5. $8\frac{9}{16}$ _____   6. $7\frac{1}{3}$ _____

7. $6\frac{2}{3}$ _____   8. $\frac{5}{7}$ _____   9. $2\frac{4}{9}$ _____

10. $5\frac{5}{11}$ _____   11. $9\frac{1}{8}$ _____   12. $9\frac{7}{8}$ _____

Name _____ Date _____

Skills Practice

Rounding Fractions and Mixed Numbers

Round each number to the nearest half.

1. $6\frac{3}{12}$ _____

2. $8\frac{12}{13}$ _____

3. $3\frac{9}{18}$ _____

4. $6\frac{3}{4}$ _____

5. $6\frac{2}{9}$ _____

6. $5\frac{2}{3}$ _____

7. $2\frac{1}{2}$ _____

8. $6\frac{3}{8}$ _____

9. $\frac{7}{8}$ _____

10. $\frac{1}{8}$ _____

11. $\frac{12}{15}$ _____

12. $3\frac{2}{9}$ _____

13. $8\frac{1}{4}$ _____

14. $\frac{11}{12}$ _____

15. $\frac{5}{6}$ _____

16. $\frac{2}{16}$ _____

17. $\frac{1}{3}$ _____

18. $2\frac{4}{5}$ _____

19. $3\frac{2}{8}$ _____

20. $9\frac{1}{5}$ _____

21. $6\frac{2}{3}$ _____

Solve.

22. Mrs. Jones is putting up blinds to fit in a window opening that is $36\frac{5}{8}$ inches wide. Should she round $36\frac{5}{8}$ up or down when deciding on the size of blinds to purchase?

_____

23. Marvin is mailing a copy of a document that is $12\frac{1}{8}$ inches long and $10\frac{1}{2}$ inches wide. Will the document fit in an envelope that is 12 inches long and $10\frac{1}{2}$ inches wide or in an envelope that is $12\frac{1}{2}$ inches long and 11 inches wide?

_____

Name _____ Date _____

Reteach

Estimating Sums and Differences

You can round mixed numbers to the nearest half to estimate sums and differences of mixed numbers. Use number lines to help you.

Estimate $5\frac{5}{8} - 2\frac{1}{5}$

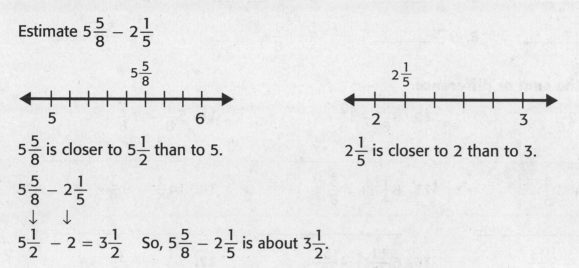

$5\frac{5}{8}$ is closer to $5\frac{1}{2}$ than to 5.

$2\frac{1}{5}$ is closer to 2 than to 3.

$5\frac{5}{8} - 2\frac{1}{5}$
↓   ↓
$5\frac{1}{2} - 2 = 3\frac{1}{2}$ So, $5\frac{5}{8} - 2\frac{1}{5}$ is about $3\frac{1}{2}$.

Show each mixed number on a number line and round it to the nearest half. Then estimate the sum or difference.

1. $3\frac{2}{5} + 4\frac{9}{10}$

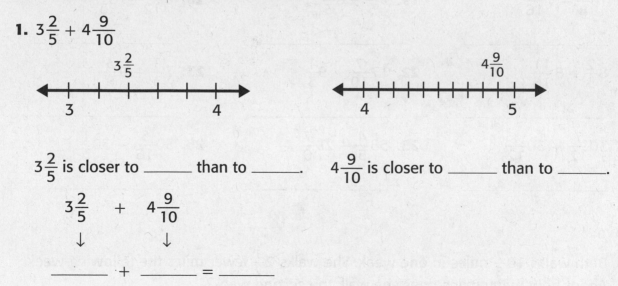

$3\frac{2}{5}$ is closer to _____ than to _____. $4\frac{9}{10}$ is closer to _____ than to _____.

$3\frac{2}{5}$ + $4\frac{9}{10}$
↓   ↓
_____ + _____ = _____

Estimate the sum or difference. You may draw number lines.

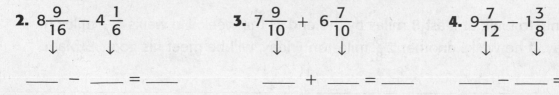

2. $8\frac{9}{16} - 4\frac{1}{6}$
↓   ↓

3. $7\frac{9}{10} + 6\frac{7}{10}$
↓   ↓

4. $9\frac{7}{12} - 1\frac{3}{8}$
↓   ↓

____ − ____ = ____   ____ + ____ = ____   ____ − ____ = ____

5-2

Skills Practice

Estimating Sums and Differences

Round to the nearest half.

1. $7\frac{3}{4}$ _____

2. $4\frac{1}{6}$ _____

3. $8\frac{2}{5}$ _____

4. $3\frac{4}{5}$ _____

5. $2\frac{9}{16}$ _____

6. $9\frac{4}{5}$ _____

7. $1\frac{7}{8}$ _____

8. $5\frac{5}{12}$ _____

Estimate the sum or difference.

9. $3\frac{7}{8} + 2\frac{1}{6}$

10. $8\frac{5}{6} - 3\frac{2}{3}$

11. $5\frac{1}{8} - 1\frac{7}{8}$

_____

_____

_____

12. $9\frac{7}{10} + 3\frac{4}{5}$

13. $6\frac{1}{4} + 7\frac{3}{8}$

14. $14\frac{1}{5} - 9\frac{3}{5}$

_____

_____

_____

15. $18\frac{5}{16} - 9\frac{13}{16}$

16. $6\frac{11}{12} + 4\frac{5}{12}$

17. $7\frac{1}{3} + 7\frac{7}{12}$

_____

_____

_____

18. $15\frac{3}{8} - 7\frac{7}{16}$

19. $9\frac{4}{5} + 6\frac{2}{3}$

20. $6\frac{11}{12} - 6\frac{1}{5}$

_____

_____

_____

21. $8\frac{2}{5} + 8\frac{11}{16}$

22. $17\frac{7}{10} - 9\frac{1}{3}$

23. $7\frac{1}{3} + 9\frac{3}{8}$

_____

_____

_____

24. $30\frac{7}{12} + 30\frac{1}{12}$

25. $58\frac{4}{5} - 29\frac{7}{8}$

26. $50\frac{5}{16} - 30\frac{1}{3}$

_____

_____

_____

Solve.

27. Beth walks $10\frac{7}{8}$ miles in one week. She walks $2\frac{1}{2}$ fewer miles the following week. About how many miles does she walk the second week?

_____

28. Jon wants to walk at least 8 miles by the end of the week. He walks $5\frac{3}{4}$ miles by Thursday. If he walks another $2\frac{5}{8}$ miles on Friday, will he meet his goal? Explain.

_____

Name _____ Date _____

Reteach

Problem-Solving Strategy

Use the *Act It Out* Strategy

Akio and Mei began the project of repainting and covering the seats of old dining room chairs. To recover one seat, they need $\frac{2}{3}$ of a yard of fabric. How much fabric do they need to buy to recover the seats of 4 chairs?

Understand	**What facts do you know?**
	There are 4 chairs to recover. $\frac{2}{3}$ of a yard of fabric is needed to cover the seat of each chair.
	What do you need to find?
	How much fabric is needed to recover the seats of 4 chairs?
Plan	Act out the problem by marking the floor to show a length of $\frac{2}{3}$ of a yard.
	Then, continue to mark $\frac{2}{3}$ of a yard of fabric until you have done this 4 times.
Solve	$\frac{2}{3} + \frac{2}{3} + \frac{2}{3} + \frac{2}{3} = \frac{8}{3} = 2\frac{2}{3}$ yards of fabric
Check	You can estimate by rounding $\frac{2}{3}$ to 1.
	Then, you have each chair needs about 1 yard of fabric.
	$1 + 1 + 1 + 1 = 4$, which is close to your answer of $2\frac{2}{3}$.

5-4

Reteach

Problem-Solving Strategy   (continued)

Solve. Use the *act it out* strategy.

1. The girls need $\frac{1}{4}$ can of paint to paint each chair. How many cans of paint will they need to paint all 4 chairs?

   _____

2. The girls found 6 more chairs that each need $\frac{2}{3}$ yard of fabric to cover the seats. How much more fabric do they need to buy?

   _____

3. Since each of the 6 chairs needs $\frac{1}{4}$ can of paint, how much more paint will they need?

   _____

4. Jean reads $\frac{1}{7}$ of her book each day. If she starts reading on Monday, on what day will she complete her book?

   _____

5. Robert lives $\frac{3}{10}$ mile from school. Al lives $\frac{7}{10}$ mile from school. Who lives farther from school? How much farther?

   _____

6. A puppy eats $\frac{1}{3}$ of a can of food at each meal. If he eats two times a day, how long will it take him to eat 4 cans of food?

   _____

Name _____ Date _____

Skills Practice

Problem-Solving Strategy

Solve. Use the *act it out* strategy.

1. The ceramics class is designing mugs with three colored stripes. The colors are red, yellow, and green. How many different ways can students in the class arrange the three colored stripes?

   _____

2. Meg and Matt are painting all 4 walls of a room. Each person is painting 2 walls. After one hour, Meg has painted $\frac{1}{2}$ of one wall, and Matt has painted 1 wall. How much longer will it take Meg to paint her 2 walls than it will take Matt to paint his?

   _____

3. Twenty-four students are in study hall. Eight more arrive. At the same time, 12 leave. Then, 16 leave and 8 more arrive. How many students are left in study hall?

   _____

4. Ellen is decorating a wall with family pictures. She has 2 pictures that are 10 inches, 2 pictures that are 8 inches, and 2 pictures that are 6 inches. If she keeps the same size pictures in rows, how many ways can she arrange the pictures?

   _____

5. Dolores has 6 quarters, 5 dimes, 4 nickels, and 10 pennies. How many different combinations of coins can she make to have $0.50?

   _____

Name _____ Date _____

Reteach

Adding and Subtracting Fractions with Unlike Denominators

When adding or subtracting fractions with unlike denominators, it helps to write the problems in vertical form.

Step 1	Step 2	Step 3
Find the least common denominator (LCD).	Rename each fraction using the LCD.	Write the problems in vertical form.
Add $\frac{7}{8} + \frac{2}{3}$. Multiples of 3: 3, 6, 9, 12, 15, 18, 21, **24**, ... Multiples of 8: 8, 16, **24**, ... The LCD is 24.	$\frac{7}{8} = \frac{21}{24}$ $\frac{2}{3} = \frac{16}{24}$	Add. $\begin{array}{r} \frac{7}{8} = \frac{21}{24} \\ + \frac{2}{3} = + \frac{16}{24} \\ \hline \frac{37}{24} = 1\frac{13}{24} \end{array}$
Subtract $\frac{3}{4} - \frac{1}{3}$. Find the LCD of $\frac{3}{4}$ and $\frac{1}{3}$. Multiples of 4: 4, 8, **12**, ... Multiples of 3: 3, 6, 9, **12**, ... The LCD of $\frac{3}{4}$ and $\frac{1}{3}$ is 12.	$\frac{3}{4} = \frac{9}{12}$ $\frac{1}{3} = \frac{4}{12}$	Subtract. $\begin{array}{r} \frac{9}{12} \\ - \frac{4}{12} \\ \hline \frac{5}{12} \end{array}$

Add or subtract. Write in simplest form.

1. $\frac{3}{8} + \frac{5}{6}$

Multiples of 8: _____

Multiples of 6: _____

LCD: _____

So, $\frac{3}{8} + \frac{5}{6} =$ _____

2. $\frac{11}{12} - \frac{3}{4}$

Multiples of 12: _____

Multiples of 4: _____

LCD: _____

So, $\frac{11}{12} - \frac{3}{4} =$ _____

Chapter Resources

5-5

Skills Practice

5NS2.3

Adding and Subtracting Fractions with Unlike Denominators

Write the addition or subtraction sentence shown by each model. Write the sum or difference in simplest form.

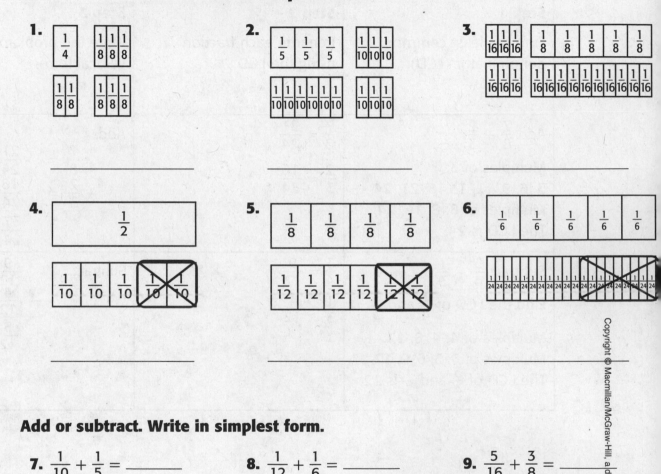

1.

$\frac{1}{4}$ | $\frac{1}{8}$ $\frac{1}{8}$ $\frac{1}{8}$

$\frac{1}{8}$ $\frac{1}{8}$ | $\frac{1}{8}$ $\frac{1}{8}$ $\frac{1}{8}$

_____

2.

$\frac{1}{5}$ $\frac{1}{5}$ $\frac{1}{5}$ | $\frac{1}{10}$ $\frac{1}{10}$ $\frac{1}{10}$

$\frac{1}{10}$ $\frac{1}{10}$ $\frac{1}{10}$ $\frac{1}{10}$ $\frac{1}{10}$ $\frac{1}{10}$ | $\frac{1}{10}$ $\frac{1}{10}$ $\frac{1}{10}$

_____

3.

$\frac{1}{16}$ $\frac{1}{16}$ $\frac{1}{16}$ | $\frac{1}{8}$ | $\frac{1}{8}$ | $\frac{1}{8}$ | $\frac{1}{8}$ | $\frac{1}{8}$

$\frac{1}{16}$ $\frac{1}{16}$ $\frac{1}{16}$ | $\frac{1}{16}$ $\frac{1}{16}$ $\frac{1}{16}$ $\frac{1}{16}$ $\frac{1}{16}$ $\frac{1}{16}$ $\frac{1}{16}$ $\frac{1}{16}$ $\frac{1}{16}$

_____

4.

$\frac{1}{2}$

$\frac{1}{10}$ $\frac{1}{10}$ $\frac{1}{10}$ $\frac{1}{10}$ $\frac{1}{10}$

_____

5.

$\frac{1}{8}$ $\frac{1}{8}$ $\frac{1}{8}$ $\frac{1}{8}$

$\frac{1}{12}$ $\frac{1}{12}$ $\frac{1}{12}$ $\frac{1}{12}$ $\frac{1}{12}$ $\frac{1}{12}$

_____

6.

$\frac{1}{6}$ $\frac{1}{6}$ $\frac{1}{6}$ $\frac{1}{6}$ $\frac{1}{6}$

$\frac{1}{24}$ ...

_____

Add or subtract. Write in simplest form.

7. $\frac{1}{10} + \frac{1}{5} =$ _____

8. $\frac{1}{12} + \frac{1}{6} =$ _____

9. $\frac{5}{16} + \frac{3}{8} =$ _____

10. $\frac{3}{4} + \frac{1}{12} =$ _____

11. $\frac{1}{2} + \frac{3}{8} =$ _____

12. $\frac{2}{3} + \frac{5}{6} =$ _____

13. $\frac{7}{12} - \frac{1}{4} =$ _____

14. $\frac{1}{2} - \frac{1}{3} =$ _____

15. $\frac{9}{10} - \frac{2}{5} =$ _____

16. $\frac{5}{8} - \frac{1}{4} =$ _____

17. $\frac{11}{20} - \frac{3}{10} =$ _____

18. $\frac{11}{12} - \frac{1}{3} =$ _____

Name _____ Date _____

Reteach

Problem-Solving Investigation

Choose the Best Strategy

Fina did a survey of how much time students spend on homework each night. Out of 16 people interviewed, $\frac{1}{2}$ spend about 1 hour on homework and $\frac{1}{4}$ spend about 45 minutes on homework. The rest spend about 30 minutes on homework. How many students spend 30 minutes on homework?

Understand	$\frac{1}{2}$ of 16 students spend 1 hour on homework.
	$\frac{1}{4}$ of 16 students spend 45 minutes on homework.
	You need to know how many people spend 30 minutes on homework.
Plan	You can use the *act it out* strategy.
	Draw 16 students.
	Cross out the students who spend 1 hour and who spend 45 minutes on homework.
	You will be left with the students who spend 30 minutes on homework.
Solve	$\frac{1}{2}$ of 16 is 8. Cross out 8 students.
	☺ ☺ ☺ ☺ ☺ ☺ ☺ ☺ ☺ ☺ ☺ ☺ ☺ ☺ ☺ ☺
	$\frac{1}{4}$ of 16 is 4. Cross out 4 more students.
	Count the students that are left. 4 students spend about 30 minutes on homework.
Check	Use math to check your work.
	$16 - 8 - 4 = 4$
	Your answer is correct.

5-6

Reteach

Problem-Solving Investigation (continued)

Use any strategy shown below to solve.

- Act it out
- Make a table
- Use logical reasoning

1. Out of the 200 students at Groves High, 50 spend 2 hours a night on homework, 25 spend 1 hour on homework, and 75 spend 45 minutes on homework. The rest spend 30 minutes on homework. How many students spend 30 minutes on homework?

   _____

2. Mrs. Jones told her class of 30 students that 8 people scored 90 on a math test, 7 people scored 80, and 10 people scored 70. How many people scored lower than 70?

   _____

3. If square tables are arranged in a restaurant so that only one person can sit on any side of the table, how many tables will it take to seat 40 people?

   _____

4. If the 40 people in the restaurant spend a total of $600 and $\frac{1}{2}$ of the 40 people spend $\frac{1}{2}$ of what the 20 other people spend, what is the least amount of money a person spends?

   _____

5. Alan bought a computer that was on sale for $568. If the computer originally cost $647, how much money did Alan save?

   _____

5-6

Skills Practice

Problem-Solving Investigation

Use any strategy shown below to solve.

- Make a table
- Use logical reasoning
- Act it out

1. In how many ways can 5 people stand in line if one of the people always has to be first in line?

   _____

2. The teacher told the class of 30 students that $\frac{1}{2}$ of them scored above an 80 on their math test. An additional $\frac{1}{3}$ of them scored at least a 70. How many of them scored below 70?

   _____

3. Alicia bought a CD player for $10 less than the regular price. If she paid $58 for the CD player, what was the regular price?

   _____

4. Miguel bought boxes of chocolates. The first box weighed $4\frac{1}{4}$ pounds, the second, $2\frac{3}{4}$, and the third, $1\frac{1}{3}$. What is the total amount of chocolate that Miguel bought?

   _____

5. After Miguel shared the chocolate with his friends, he had $3\frac{5}{8}$ pounds left. Then, he gave $2\frac{3}{4}$ pounds to his mother. Now, how much does he have?

   _____

6. The first $\frac{1}{5}$ mile of a $\frac{3}{4}$-mile path through a rose garden is paved with bricks. How much of the path is not paved with bricks?

   _____

Name _____ Date _____

Reteach

Adding and Subtracting Mixed Numbers

Add $1\frac{7}{8} + 1\frac{1}{2}$.

Rename the addends using their LCD.

Multiples of 8: **8**, 16, 24, . . .

Multiples of 2: 2, 4, 6, **8**, . . .

The LCD of $1\frac{7}{8}$ and $1\frac{1}{2}$ is 8.

Show $1\frac{7}{8}$ and $1\frac{1}{2}$ using eighths as a denominator.

$$1\frac{7}{8} \rightarrow 1\frac{7}{8}$$
$$+ 1\frac{1}{2} \rightarrow 1\frac{4}{8}$$
$$\overline{}$$
$$2\frac{11}{8} = 2 + 1\frac{3}{8} \text{ or } 3\frac{3}{8}$$

Add the ones.
Then count the eighths.

Subtract $2\frac{3}{4} - 1\frac{5}{8}$.

Find the LCD of $\frac{3}{4}$ and $\frac{5}{8}$.

Multiples of 4: 4, **8**,
Multiples of 8: **8**, . . .
The LCD of $\frac{3}{4}$ and $\frac{5}{8}$ is 8.

Rename $2\frac{3}{4}$ so the fraction part is in eighths. Subtract the ones. Then subtract the eighths.

$$2\frac{3}{4}$$
$$\downarrow$$
$$2\frac{6}{8} - 1\frac{5}{8} = 1\frac{1}{8}$$

Add or subtract. Write in simplest form.

1. $2\frac{5}{8} + 1\frac{3}{4} =$ _____

2. $1\frac{3}{5} + 2\frac{7}{10} =$ _____

3. $6\frac{4}{5} - 1\frac{7}{10} =$ _____

4. $3\frac{3}{8} - 1\frac{1}{4} =$ _____

Name _____ Date _____

Skills Practice

Adding and Subtracting Mixed Numbers

Add or subtract. Write in simplest form.

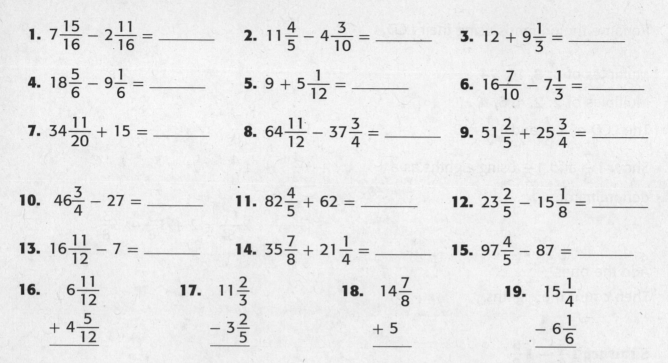

1. $7\frac{15}{16} - 2\frac{11}{16} = $ _____

2. $11\frac{4}{5} - 4\frac{3}{10} = $ _____

3. $12 + 9\frac{1}{3} = $ _____

4. $18\frac{5}{6} - 9\frac{1}{6} = $ _____

5. $9 + 5\frac{1}{12} = $ _____

6. $16\frac{7}{10} - 7\frac{1}{3} = $ _____

7. $34\frac{11}{20} + 15 = $ _____

8. $64\frac{11}{12} - 37\frac{3}{4} = $ _____

9. $51\frac{2}{5} + 25\frac{3}{4} = $ _____

10. $46\frac{3}{4} - 27 = $ _____

11. $82\frac{4}{5} + 62 = $ _____

12. $23\frac{2}{5} - 15\frac{1}{8} = $ _____

13. $16\frac{11}{12} - 7 = $ _____

14. $35\frac{7}{8} + 21\frac{1}{4} = $ _____

15. $97\frac{4}{5} - 87 = $ _____

16. $6\frac{11}{12}$
  $+ 4\frac{5}{12}$
  _____

17. $11\frac{2}{3}$
  $- 3\frac{2}{5}$
  _____

18. $14\frac{7}{8}$
  $+ 5$
  _____

19. $15\frac{1}{4}$
  $- 6\frac{1}{6}$
  _____

20. A grocery bag will hold $8\frac{5}{8}$ pounds of oranges. Kyle puts 3 pounds of oranges in the bag. How many more pounds of oranges can he put in the bag?

_____

21. Sara needs $2\frac{7}{8}$ pounds of grapes for a salad. She buys a bag of grapes that weighs only $1\frac{1}{2}$ pounds. How many more pounds of grapes does she need?

_____

22. Keith is making canvas tent. He needs $12\frac{3}{4}$ yards of beige canvas for the top and $8\frac{2}{5}$ of green canvas for the bottom. How many yards of canvas does he need in all?

_____

Name _____ Date _____

Reteach

5NS2.1

Multiplying Decimals by Whole Numbers

To multiply a whole number by a decimal, multiply as you would with whole numbers. Then count the number of decimal places in each factor. Write the same number of decimal places in the product.

- Multiply: 7×3.28

- Estimate: $7 \times 3 = 21$

  $$3.\mathbf{28} \leftarrow 2 \text{ decimal places}$$
  $$\underline{\times \quad 7}$$
  $$22.\mathbf{96} \leftarrow 2 \text{ decimal places}$$

- Compare the actual product and the estimated product:
  22.96 is close to 21,
  so 22.96 is a reasonable answer.

- Multiply: 3×0.09

- Estimate: $3 \times 0 = 0$

  $$0.\mathbf{09} \leftarrow 2 \text{ decimal places}$$
  $$\underline{\times \quad 3}$$
  $$0.\mathbf{27} \leftarrow 2 \text{ decimal places}$$

- Compare the actual product and the estimated product:
  0.27 is close to 0,
  so 0.27 is a reasonable answer.

Write the number of decimal places. Multiply.

1. $\begin{array}{r} 0.9 \\ \times\ 9 \\ \hline \end{array}$ ← _____ decimal place(s)

    ← _____ decimal place(s)

2. $\begin{array}{r} \$3.92 \\ \times\ \quad 5 \\ \hline \end{array}$ ← _____ decimal place(s)

    ← _____ decimal place(s)

3. $\begin{array}{r} 3.79 \\ \times\ 8 \\ \hline \end{array}$ ← _____ decimal place(s)

    ← _____ decimal place(s)

4. $\begin{array}{r} 21.8 \\ \times\ 4 \\ \hline \end{array}$ ← _____ decimal place(s)

    ← _____ decimal place(s)

Multiply.

5. $\begin{array}{r} 7.2 \\ \times\ 6 \\ \hline \end{array}$

6. $\begin{array}{r} 0.67 \\ \times\ 2 \\ \hline \end{array}$

7. $\begin{array}{r} \$1.75 \\ \times\ 7 \\ \hline \end{array}$

8. $\begin{array}{r} 68.7 \\ \times\ 4 \\ \hline \end{array}$

9. $\begin{array}{r} 98.5 \\ \times\ 8 \\ \hline \end{array}$

10. $\begin{array}{r} 8.5 \\ \times\ 3 \\ \hline \end{array}$

11. $\begin{array}{r} 1.08 \\ \times\ 9 \\ \hline \end{array}$

12. $\begin{array}{r} 7.9 \\ \times\ 41 \\ \hline \end{array}$

13. $\begin{array}{r} 2.6 \\ \times\ 72 \\ \hline \end{array}$

14. $\begin{array}{r} \$23.54 \\ \times\ \quad 5 \\ \hline \end{array}$

Name _____ Date _____

Skills Practice

Multiplying Decimals by Whole Numbers

Multiply.

1. $\begin{array}{r} 1.6 \\ \times\ 8 \\ \hline \end{array}$

2. $\begin{array}{r} 2.83 \\ \times\ 7 \\ \hline \end{array}$

3. $\begin{array}{r} 14.7 \\ \times\ 24 \\ \hline \end{array}$

4. $\begin{array}{r} 3.75 \\ \times\ 100 \\ \hline \end{array}$

5. $\begin{array}{r} 2.09 \\ \times\ 8 \\ \hline \end{array}$

6. $\begin{array}{r} 12.8 \\ \times\ 10 \\ \hline \end{array}$

7. $\begin{array}{r} 2.55 \\ \times\ 42 \\ \hline \end{array}$

8. $\begin{array}{r} 4.7 \\ \times\ 85 \\ \hline \end{array}$

9. $\begin{array}{r} \$34.99 \\ \times\ 4 \\ \hline \end{array}$

10. $\begin{array}{r} 147.4 \\ \times\ 2 \\ \hline \end{array}$

11. $0.8 \times 5 =$ _____

12. $6 \times \$1.79 =$ _____

13. $2.46 \times 10 =$ _____

14. $10.4 \times 1,000 =$ _____

15. $2.3 \times 38 =$ _____

16. $57 \times 5.18 =$ _____

Write each number in standard form.

17. 6.1×10^2 _____

18. 1.184×10^2 _____

19. 2.495×10^2 _____

20. 5.267×10^5 _____

21. 3.205×10^3 _____

22. 1.2×10^1 _____

23. Each Sunday during his nine-week summer vacation, Ray buys a newspaper. The Sunday paper costs $1.85. How much did Ray spend on the Sunday newspaper during his vacation?

_____

24. One Sunday, Ray weighed the newspaper. It weighed 2.7 lb. If each Sunday newspaper weighs the same, how many pounds of newspaper will Ray recycle if he buys the Sunday paper for 50 weeks?

_____

Name _____ Date _____

Reteach

Multiplying Decimals

To multiply a decimal by a decimal, multiply as you would whole numbers. Then count the total number of decimal places in both factors. Write the same number of decimal places in the product. Sometimes you have to write zeros to place the decimal in the product.

Multiply: 4.7×2.63

Estimate: $5 \times 3 = 15$

$$
\begin{array}{r}
2.\mathbf{63} \leftarrow 2 \text{ decimal places} \\
\times\ 4.\mathbf{7} \leftarrow 1 \text{ decimal places} \\
\hline
1841 \\
+\ 10520 \\
\hline
12.\mathbf{361}\ 3 \text{ decimal places}
\end{array}
$$

Compare the product and the estimate. 12.361 is close to 15, so 12.361 is a reasonable answer.

Multiply: 0.5×0.07

$$
\begin{array}{r}
0.07 \leftarrow 2 \text{ decimal places} \\
\times\ 0.5 \leftarrow 1 \text{ decimal places} \\
\hline
0.\mathbf{0}35 \leftarrow 3 \text{ decimal places}
\end{array}
$$
↑

Write a zero to place the decimal in the product.

Write the number of decimal places. Multiply.

1. $0.9 \leftarrow$ _____ decimal place(s)
$\times\ 0.5 \leftarrow$ _____ decimal place(s)
$\leftarrow$ _____ decimal place(s)

2. $0.89 \leftarrow$ _____ decimal place(s)
$\times\ 0.9 \leftarrow$ _____ decimal place(s)
$\leftarrow$ _____ decimal place(s)

Multiply. Estimate to check if your answer is reasonable.

3.   0.8
     $\times\ 0.7$

4.   2.5
     $\times\ 0.6$

5.   3.67
     $\times\ 0.49$

6.   8.73
     $\times\ 0.5$

7.   9.2
     $\times\ 6.1$

8.   54.06
     $\times\ 0.2$

9.   7.13
     $\times\ 1.9$

10.   9.23
     $\times\ 4.8$

Name _____ Date _____

Skills Practice

Multiplying Decimals

Multiply.

1.	0.6 $\times$ 0.8	2.	0.5 $\times$ 0.6	3.	1.7 $\times$ 0.9	4.	2.61 $\times$ 0.4	5.	2.09 $\times$ 0.3

6.	5.18 $\times$ 2.7	7.	6.09 $\times$ 8.6	8.	37.24 $\times$ 3.1	9.	218.7 $\times$ 4.8	10.	432.1 $\times$ 1.2

11. $0.9 \times 0.7 =$ _____

12. $0.16 \times 0.6 =$ _____

13. $7.4 \times 0.4 =$ _____

14. $3.47 \times 0.9 =$ _____

15. $4.35 \times 1.7 =$ _____

16. $58.2 \times 6.8 =$ _____

17. $3.06 \times 9.1 =$ _____

18. $94.2 \times 2.5 =$ _____

19. $17.64 \times 3.2 =$ _____

20. $41.38 \times 9.7 =$ _____

Find the number that makes each problem true.

21.	39.8 $\times$ 0.7 27.☐6	22.	46.87 $\times$ 0.5 23.☐35	23.	2.3 $\times$ 1.8 ☐.14	24.	57.8 $\times$ 0.7 4☐.46

Problem Solving

25. Beth works as a lifeguard at a city park. She earns $9.50 per hour and works 7.5 hours each day. How much does she earn each day?

_____

26. The cost of renting a pedal boat at the city park is $6.25 per hour. Jason rented a boat for 1.5 hours. To the nearest cent, how much did the pedal boat rental cost?

_____

Name _____ Date _____

Reteach
Problem-Solving Strategy

Check for Reasonableness

Erica takes a package of two paperback books to the post office. The package weighs 16 ounces. Erica estimates that the package weighs about 300 pounds. Is her estimate reasonable?

Step 1 Understand	**Be sure you understand the problem.** • What facts do you know? You know how many ounces the package weighs. • What do you need to find? You need to know whether Erica's estimate is reasonable.
Step 2 Plan	**Make a plan.** You want to compare the weight of the package to something that you know weighs about 300 pounds.
Step 3 Solve	**Carry out your plan.** A professional football player might weigh between 200 and 300 pounds. So, 300 pounds is much heavier than a package of two books. Therefore, the estimate is not reasonable. Erica multiplied to change a smaller unit to a larger one. She should have divided. 16 ÷ 16 = 1 ← Remember: 1 pound = 16 ounces.
Step 4 Check	**Check for Reasonableness** • Does your answer make sense? • Did you answer the question? Yes. Erica's estimate was not reasonable. You found the mistake she made.

Is each estimate reasonable? Explain.

1. Jerry measures the hallway and finds that it is 240 feet long. He estimates that he will need a carpet that is 20 inches long in order to cover the hallway. Is Jerry's estimate reasonable? (*Hint*: 1 foot equals 12 inches)

_____

_____

Reteach *(continued)*

2. Leslie's computer weighs 165 ounces. She estimates that it weighs about 10 pounds. Is Leslie's estimate reasonable?

_____

_____

3. Rocky measures his bedroom and finds that it is 10 feet wide and 14 feet long. He thinks he can easily fit a desk that is 75 inches long in his room. Is this a reasonable guess?

_____

_____

4. Haruko wants to make a dress. The pattern she is using called for 2 yards of material. Haruko estimates that she will need to buy 2 feet of material. Is her estimate reasonable? (*Hint*: 1 yard equals 3 feet)

_____

_____

5. Eli weighs 900 ounces. He guesses that he can get on a ride at the amusement park that allows children from 30 to 80 pounds. Is his estimate reasonable?

_____

_____

6-3

Skills Practice

Problem-Solving Strategy

Check for Reasonableness

Is each estimate reasonable? Explain.

1. Sandra needs to buy a phone cord that will reach a distance of at least 12 yards. At the store, all of the packages are marked in feet. Sandra estimates that the package with 40 feet of cord will be enough. Is her estimate reasonable? (*Hint*: 1 yard equals 3 feet)

   _____

   _____

2. Kyle and Julie are watching a television program on weightlifting. A man is going to lift 210 pounds. Julie comments that he is going to lift 4,000 ounces. Is her estimate reasonable? (*Hint*: 1 pound equals 16 ounces)

   _____

   _____

3. Ryan and Tyler are going to the pet shop to buy 12 cans of dog food. They are trying to decide whether they should take their wagon to help carry the dog food home. The cans weigh 15 ounces each. They estimate that the dog food will weigh 10 pounds. Is the estimate reasonable?

   _____

   _____

4. Nicole is trying out a new recipe. The recipe calls for 4 pints of broth. Nicole has only a 1-cup measuring cup. She estimates that she will need 16 cups of broth. Is her estimate reasonable? (*Hint*: 1 pint equals 2 cups)

   _____

   _____

Name _____ Date _____

Reteach

Dividing Decimals by Whole Numbers

Dividing decimals is similar to dividing whole numbers, except that you don't write a remainder in the quotient. You may have to write one or more zeros in the dividend and keep dividing.

Divide 5.1 ÷ 4.

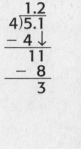

Place the decimal point in the quotient. Divide as with whole numbers. The remainder is not 0, so keep dividing.

```
      1.275
  4)5.100
   - 4 ↓↓↓
     11↓↓
    - 8↓↓
      30↓
    - 28↓
      20
    - 20
       0
```

Write zeros in the dividend and keep dividing until the remainder is 0.

Multiply to check.
1.275   ← quotient
×   4   ← divisor
5.100
5.100 = 5.1   ← dividend

Divide. Multiply to check.

1.

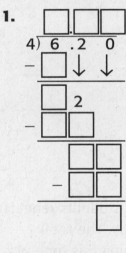

```
4) 6 . 2  0
```

Check:

2.

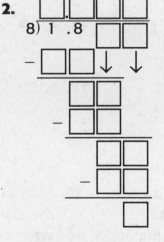

```
8) 1 . 8
```

Check:

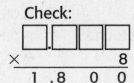

```
×           8
1 . 8  0  0
```

3.

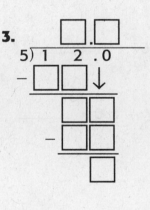

```
5) 1   2 . 0
```

Check:

```
×         5
1 2 . 0
```

4. 8)45.6

5. 6)21.3

6. 4)18

7. 34)7.82

8. 15)34.65

9. 56)47.6

6-4

Skills Practice

5NS2.1, 5NS2.2

Dividing Decimals by Whole Numbers

Divide. Round each quotient to the nearest hundredth if necessary.

1. $3\overline{)2.19}$

2. $6\overline{)3.63}$

3. $5\overline{)12}$

4. $8\overline{)18.2}$

5. $6\overline{)22}$

6. $4\overline{)2.06}$

7. $8\overline{)16.8}$

8. $10\overline{)118}$

9. $6\overline{)14.23}$

10. $23\overline{)32.2}$

11. $62\overline{)651}$

12. $56\overline{)13.5}$

13. $8.01 \div 9 =$ _____

14. $6.48 \div 40 =$ _____

15. $13.64 \div 7 =$ _____

16. $240.5 \div 64 =$ _____

17. $627 \div 100 =$ _____

18. $30.87 \div 4 =$ _____

Solve.

19. Twelve students each ordered a different meal from a fast-food restaurant as part of a science project. When they finished eating, they weighed all the packaging. They found that the packaging weighed a total of 2.88 lb. What was the average weight of the packaging from each meal?

_____

20. Later in the year, the students repeated the experiment exactly. The total weight of the packaging this time was 2.06 lb. To the nearest hundredth of a pound, what was the new average weight of the packaging?

_____

Name _____   Date _____

Reteach

Dividing by Decimals

To divide when the divisor is a decimal, multiply the divisor by the least power of ten that will make it a whole number. Then multiply the dividend by the same power of ten.

Divide 3.66 ÷ 0.6.

Multiply the divisor by the power of 10 that makes it a whole number.

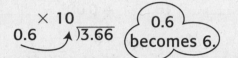

Multiply the dividend by the same number. Rewrite the problem.

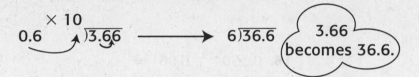

Divide as with whole numbers. Place the decimal point above its new position in the dividend.

$$
\begin{array}{r}
6.1 \\
6\overline{)36.6} \\
-36 \\
\hline
06 \\
-\ 6 \\
\hline
0
\end{array}
$$
so, 3.66 ÷ 0.6 = 6.1

Divide.

1. 0.08)3.684

2. 0.4)26

3. 0.25)10

4. 0.12)6.6

5. 1.2)0.312

6. 0.35)8.4

7. 8.4)548

8. 0.001)0.8

9. 0.42)14.7

Name _____ Date _____

Skills Practice

Dividing by Decimals

Divide.

1. $3.4\overline{)12.92}$ 2. $0.8\overline{)26.08}$ 3. $0.67\overline{)3.618}$ 4. $0.03\overline{)0.294}$

5. $82.65 \div 9.5 =$ _____   6. $0.48 \div 0.6 =$ _____   7. $34.281 \div 0.09 =$ _____

8. $7.224 \div 0.08 =$ _____   9. $224 \div 0.7 =$ _____   10. $5.1 \div 0.003 =$ _____

11. $0.07\overline{)0.868}$ 12. $0.046\overline{)3.0084}$ 13. $2.5\overline{)8.79}$ 14. $1.3\overline{)99.06}$

Divide.

15. $1.44 \div 0.45 =$ _____   16. $0.3904 \div 0.061 =$ _____

17. $0.5341 \div 0.49 =$ _____   18. $42 \div 0.06 =$ _____

19. $12 \div 0.005 =$ _____   20. $32.2 \div 0.46 =$ _____

21. $63.96 \div 7.8 =$ _____   22. $242 \div 0.55 =$ _____

23. $\$8.46 \div 1.2 =$ _____   24. $134.13 \div 5.1 =$ _____

25. $41.07 \div 0.5 =$ _____   26. $\$36.12 \div 3.5 =$ _____

Solve.

27. One type of motor-driven camera can take a picture every 0.06 second. While taking some action pictures, a photographer let the camera run for 3.6 seconds. How many pictures did the camera take?

_____

Name _____ Date _____

Reteach

5MR1.1, 5NS2.1

Problem-Solving Investigation

Choose the Best Strategy

Dominique made invitations on her computer for a party. She distributed $\frac{1}{2}$ of the invitations, while her friend gave out 11. There are 5 more invitations that need to be delivered. How many invitations were there to begin with?

Step 1
Understand
	Be sure you understand the problem.
	Read carefully.
	What facts do you know?
	    • Dominique distributed _____ of the invitations.
	    • Her friend gave out _____ invitations.
	    • There are _____ invitations that still need to be delivered.
	What do you need to find?
	    • The _____ there were to begin with.

Step 2 Plan Choose a Strategy • Make an organized list • Determine reasonable answers • Use logical reasoning	**Make a plan.** Choose a strategy. You can work backward to solve the problem. Start with the number of invitations that still need to be delivered. Add the number of invitations that Dominique's friend gave out. Double the sum to find the number of invitations there were to begin with.

Reteach

Problem-Solving Investigation (continued)

Step 3 Solve	**Carry out your plan.** Add the number of invitations that still need to be delivered and the number of invitations that Dominique's friend gave out. _____ + _____ = _____ So, there were _____ invitations left after Dominique distributed her invitations. Think: Dominique distributed _____ of the invitations. If there are _____ left over, they are the other half. Add the number of invitations that Dominique distributed to the number of invitations left after she distributed hers. _____ + _____ = _____ How many invitations were there to begin with? _____
Step 4 Check	**Is the solution reasonable?** Reread the problem. How can you check your answer by working forward? _____ _____ _____ _____

Practice

1. The coach gives uniforms to $\frac{1}{2}$ of the players on a soccer team. Brad helps out, giving uniforms to 3 players. James gives the remaining uniforms to 5 players. How many players are on the soccer team?

_____

2. Leslie is $\frac{1}{2}$ as old as Carey. Carey is 2 years older than Jennifer. Jennifer is 18 years old. How old is Leslie?

_____

6-6

5MR1.1, 5NS2.1

Skills Practice

Problem-Solving Investigation

Solve. Use any strategy.

1. Matt bought a tennis racket that usually costs $73.95. He had a coupon for a discount of *d* dollars. The net price of the racket with the discount was *c* dollars. Write an equation that represents the relationship between the net price and the discount.

_____

2. Use the equation you wrote for exercise 1 to find the net price if the discount was $7.50.

_____

3. Brooke is making a necklace in which the first, fifth, ninth, and thirteenth beads are blue and the rest of the first 15 beads are not blue. If the necklace continues this pattern and has 50 beads in all, how many of them will be blue?

_____

Strategy: _____

4. Create a problem that you could solve by making an organized list. Share your work with others.

_____

5. Ms. Gonzaga ordered a bookcase that cost $89.45. The delivery fee was *f* dollars. The cost with the delivery fee was *t* dollars. Write an equation that represents the relationship between the delivery fee and the cost with the delivery fee.

_____

6. Use the equation you wrote for exercise 5 to find the total cost if the delivery fee was $29.95.

_____

7. A salesman spends $89 per night for 5 nights at a hotel, $219.49 for transportation, and $137.71 for food. What are his total travel expenses?

_____

Strategy: _____

Name _____ Date _____

Reteach

5MR2.5, 5NS2.5

Estimating Products of Fractions

To estimate a fraction of a whole number or mixed number, you can round the whole number or mixed number to a multiple of the denominator.

Estimate $\frac{5}{6} \times 44$.

Think: $\frac{5}{6} \times 42$

Round the whole number to the closest multiple of the denominator.
42 is close to 44.

$42 \div 6 = 7$
$5 \times 7 = 35$

So, $\frac{5}{6} \times 44$ is about 35.

Estimate each product.

1. $\frac{1}{5} \times 27$

   Denominator of fraction: _____

   Multiples of denominator: _____, _____, _____, _____, _____, _____

   Estimate: $\frac{1}{5} \times$ _____ = _____

2. $30 \times \frac{7}{8}$

   _____

3. $\frac{2}{3} \times 17$

   _____

4. $43 \times \frac{3}{5}$

   _____

5. $\frac{1}{6} \times 28$

   _____

6. $\frac{3}{4} \times 37$

   _____

7. $29 \times \frac{3}{8}$

   _____

8. $\frac{4}{5} \times 34$

   _____

9. $\frac{5}{6} \times 43$

   _____

10. $\frac{9}{10} \times 28$

    _____

11. $39 \times \frac{7}{8}$

    _____

12. $\frac{2}{3} \times 20$

    _____

13. $\frac{1}{3} \times 44$

    _____

Name _____ Date _____

Skills Practice

Estimating Products of Fractions

Estimate each product.

1. $\frac{1}{2} \times 13$

2. $7 \times 3\frac{1}{4}$

3. $\frac{4}{7} \times 8\frac{1}{9}$

_____

_____

_____

4. $\frac{5}{6} \times 23$

5. $21\frac{8}{9} \times \frac{5}{12}$

6. $17 \times \frac{2}{5}$

_____

_____

_____

7. $2\frac{1}{6} \times 9\frac{3}{4}$

8. $13\frac{7}{8} \times \frac{3}{8}$

9. $6 \times 8\frac{4}{5}$

_____

_____

_____

10. $31 \times \frac{2}{3}$

11. $\frac{2}{5} \times 24\frac{1}{4}$

12. $3\frac{5}{6} \times 4\frac{2}{3}$

_____

_____

_____

13. $\frac{7}{8} \times 62$

14. $1\frac{11}{12} \times 9\frac{1}{5}$

15. $34 \times \frac{1}{6}$

_____

_____

_____

Estimate to compare. Write >, < or =.

16. $34 \times \frac{3}{4}$ ◯ $59\frac{5}{6} \times \frac{4}{9}$

17. $\frac{3}{8} \times 33$ ◯ $\frac{5}{8} \times 10\frac{1}{4}$

_____

_____

Solve.

18. Teresa rode $6\frac{7}{10}$ miles on her bike in one hour. If she continues at this pace, about how far could she ride in 5 hours?

_____

19. Chan is riding his bike on a 48-mile cross-country course. He knows that $\frac{2}{5}$ of the course is uphill. About how many miles will Chan have to ride uphill?

_____

Name _____ Date _____

Reteach

Multiplying Fractions

To multiply a fraction by a fraction, multiply the numerators and the denominators. Then simplify the product.

$$\frac{2}{3} \times \frac{5}{8} = \frac{2 \times 5}{3 \times 8} = \frac{10}{24} = \frac{10 \div 2}{24 \div 2} = \frac{5}{12}$$

When the numerator and denominator of either fraction have a common factor, you can simplify before you multiply. Divide the numerator and the denominator by their GCF (greatest common factor).

Look at the numerator, 2, and the denominator, 8. Their GCF is 2, so divide both 2 and 8 by 2.

$$\frac{2}{3} \times \frac{5}{8}$$

Look at the other numerator, 5, and the other denominator, 3. Their GCF is 1, so dividing won't change the answer.

Now multiply. The product is already in simplest form.

$$\frac{\overset{1}{\cancel{2}}}{3} \times \frac{5}{\underset{4}{\cancel{8}}} = \frac{1 \times 5}{3 \times 4} = \frac{5}{12}$$

Multiply. Write in simplest form.

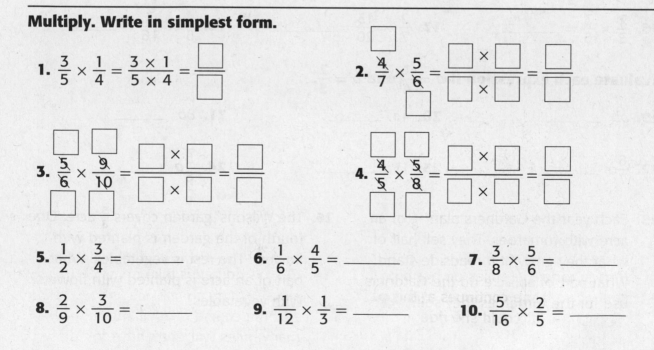

1. $\dfrac{3}{5} \times \dfrac{1}{4} = \dfrac{3 \times 1}{5 \times 4} = \dfrac{\square}{\square}$

2. $\dfrac{4}{7} \times \dfrac{5}{6} = \dfrac{\square \times \square}{\square \times \square} = \dfrac{\square}{\square}$

3. $\dfrac{5}{6} \times \dfrac{9}{10} = \dfrac{\square \times \square}{\square \times \square} = \dfrac{\square}{\square}$

4. $\dfrac{4}{5} \times \dfrac{5}{8} = \dfrac{\square \times \square}{\square \times \square} = \dfrac{\square}{\square}$

5. $\dfrac{1}{2} \times \dfrac{3}{4} =$ _____

6. $\dfrac{1}{6} \times \dfrac{4}{5} =$ _____

7. $\dfrac{3}{8} \times \dfrac{5}{6} =$ _____

8. $\dfrac{2}{9} \times \dfrac{3}{10} =$ _____

9. $\dfrac{1}{12} \times \dfrac{1}{3} =$ _____

10. $\dfrac{5}{16} \times \dfrac{2}{5} =$ _____

6-8

Skills Practice

Multiplying Fractions

5NS2.5

Multiply. Write in simplest form.

1. $\frac{1}{2} \times \frac{3}{8} =$ _____

2. $\frac{7}{12} \times \frac{4}{5} =$ _____

3. $\frac{3}{4} \times \frac{1}{9} =$ _____

4. $\frac{4}{9} \times \frac{5}{6} =$ _____

5. $\frac{3}{4} \times \frac{1}{3} =$ _____

6. $\frac{5}{8} \times \frac{3}{10} =$ _____

7. $\frac{2}{9} \times \frac{1}{2} =$ _____

8. $\frac{3}{5} \times \frac{3}{8} =$ _____

9. $\frac{8}{9} \times \frac{5}{16} =$ _____

10. $\frac{1}{5} \times \frac{7}{12} =$ _____

11. $\frac{3}{10} \times \frac{1}{4} =$ _____

12. $\frac{5}{7} \times \frac{7}{9} =$ _____

13. $\frac{9}{20} \times \frac{2}{3} =$ _____

14. $\frac{3}{5} \times \frac{7}{12} =$ _____

15. $\frac{1}{16} \times \frac{8}{9} =$ _____

16. $\frac{2}{3} \times \frac{3}{5} =$ _____

17. $\frac{2}{7} \times \frac{13}{20} =$ _____

18. $\frac{4}{5} \times \frac{7}{16} =$ _____

Evaluate each expression if $a = \frac{1}{4}$ and $b = \frac{2}{5}$.

19. ab _____

20. $4a$ _____

21. $8b$ _____

22. $\frac{6}{7}a$ _____

23. $15b$ _____

24. $\frac{5}{6}b$ _____

25. Each year the Gardners plant $\frac{7}{8}$ of an acre with tomatoes. They sell half of what they grow at a roadside stand. What part of an acre do the Gardners use for the tomatoes they sell?

26. The Wilsons' garden covers $\frac{5}{8}$ acre. One fourth of the garden is planted with flowers. The rest is vegetables. What part of an acre is planted with flowers? With vegetables?

_____

_____

Name _____ Date _____

Reteach

Dividing Fractions

Dividing by a fraction is the same as multiplying by its reciprocal.

Divide $\frac{7}{8} \div \frac{3}{4}$.

Step 1: Find the reciprocal of the divisor.

The divisor is $\frac{3}{4}$.

The reciprocal of $\frac{3}{4}$ is $\frac{4}{3}$.

Step 2: Multiply by the reciprocal of the divisor.

$\frac{7}{\underset{2}{8}} \times \frac{\overset{1}{4}}{3} = \frac{7}{6}$

Step 3: Simplify.

$\frac{7}{6} = 1\frac{1}{6}$

Divide $\frac{5}{8} \div 3$.

Step 1: Find the reciprocal of the divisor.

The divisor is 3, or $\frac{3}{1}$.

The reciprocal of $\frac{3}{1}$ is $\frac{1}{3}$.

Step 2: Multiply by the reciprocal of the divisor.

$\frac{5}{8} \times \frac{1}{3} = \frac{5}{24}$

Divide. Write each quotient in simplest form.

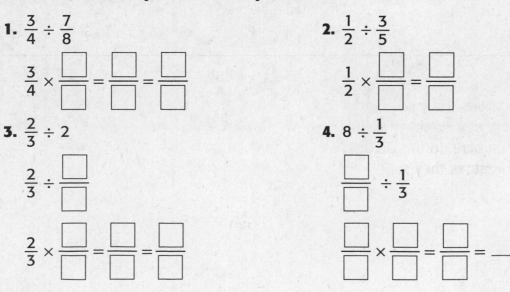

1. $\frac{3}{4} \div \frac{7}{8}$

$\frac{3}{4} \times \frac{\square}{\square} = \frac{\square}{\square} = \frac{\square}{\square}$

2. $\frac{1}{2} \div \frac{3}{5}$

$\frac{1}{2} \times \frac{\square}{\square} = \frac{\square}{\square}$

3. $\frac{2}{3} \div 2$

$\frac{2}{3} \div \frac{\square}{\square}$

$\frac{2}{3} \times \frac{\square}{\square} = \frac{\square}{\square} = \frac{\square}{\square}$

4. $8 \div \frac{1}{3}$

$\frac{\square}{\square} \div \frac{1}{3}$

$\frac{\square}{\square} \times \frac{\square}{\square} = \frac{\square}{\square} = \underline{\quad}$

Name _____EHC_____ Date _____

Skills Practice

Dividing Fractions

5NS2.5

Find the reciprocal of each number.

1. $\frac{2}{3}$ $\frac{3}{2}$

2. $\frac{3}{5}$ $\frac{5}{3}$

3. $\frac{1}{7}$ $\frac{7}{1}$

4. $\frac{5}{6}$ $\frac{6}{5}$

5. 3 $\frac{1}{3}$

6. $\frac{7}{8}$ $\frac{8}{7}$

7. $\frac{1}{4}$ $\frac{4}{1}$

8. $\frac{11}{12}$ $\frac{12}{11}$

9. 5 $\frac{1}{5}$

10. 2 $\frac{1}{2}$

11. $\frac{5}{4}$ $\frac{4}{5}$

12. 8 $\frac{1}{8}$

Divide. Write in simplest form.

13. $\frac{1}{3} \div \frac{1}{4} =$ $1\frac{1}{3}$

14. $\frac{1}{2} \div \frac{4}{5} =$ $\frac{5}{8}$

15. $\frac{2}{3} \div 8 =$ $\frac{1}{12}$

16. $\frac{8}{9} \div \frac{2}{3} =$ $1\frac{1}{3}$

17. $\frac{5}{8} \div \frac{3}{4} =$ $\frac{5}{6}$

18. $\frac{3}{4} \div \frac{2}{5} =$ $1\frac{7}{8}$

19. $\frac{5}{6} \div 5 =$ $\frac{1}{6}$

20. $\frac{2}{5} \div \frac{4}{5} =$ $\frac{1}{2}$

21. $\frac{1}{3} \div 9 =$ $\frac{1}{27}$

22. $\frac{5}{8} \div \frac{1}{4} =$ $2\frac{1}{2}$

23. $\frac{4}{5} \div 7 =$ $\frac{4}{35}$

24. $\frac{1}{3} \div \frac{2}{3} =$ $\frac{1}{2}$

25. $6 \div \frac{1}{4}$ 24

26. $\frac{7}{9} \div 2$ $\frac{7}{18}$

27. $\frac{3}{8} \div \frac{1}{2}$ $\frac{3}{4}$

28. It takes $\frac{7}{8}$ inch of wire to make a small paper clip. How many small paper clips can be made from a piece of wire that is 14 inches long?

Name __EhC__ Date _____

Reteach

5NS1.5

Ordering Integers

An **integer** is a whole number or its opposite. You can use a number line to show integers.

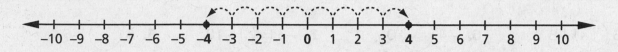

Opposite integers, like −4 and 4, are the same distance from 0. For two integers on a number line, the greater integer is farther to the right.

You can use a number line to compare integers.
Compare −2 and 1. You can see that 1 is farther to the right.

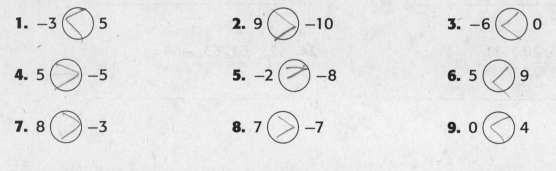

So, 1 > −2 or −2 < 1.

Write < or > to make a true sentence.

1. −3 ⟨<⟩ 5   **2.** 9 ⟨>⟩ −10   **3.** −6 ⟨<⟩ 0

4. 5 ⟨>⟩ −5   **5.** −2 ⟨>⟩ −8   **6.** 5 ⟨<⟩ 9

7. 8 ⟨>⟩ −3   **8.** 7 ⟨>⟩ −7   **9.** 0 ⟨<⟩ 4

Order each set of integers from least to greatest.

10. 2, −3, 0 ___−3, 0, 2___   **11.** −2, 3, −4 ___−4, −2, 3___

12. −14, 14, −17, 28 ___−17, −14, 14, 28___ **13.** −42, 44, −47, 48 ___−47, −42, 44, 48___

14. −62, 58, −17, 13 ___−62, −17, 13, 58___ **15.** 72, −77, −79, 71 ___−79, −77, 71, 72___

Name _____ Date _____

Skills Practice

5NS1.5

Ordering Integers

Write < or > to make a true sentence.

1. −2 ◯ 4
2. 3 ◯ −7
3. −6 ◯ −9
4. −5 ◯ 1

5. 6 ◯ −8
6. −4 ◯ 0
7. −3 ◯ −10
8. 6 ◯ −6

9. −12 ◯ −10
10. 13 ◯ −17
11. 0 ◯ −17
12. −14 ◯ 21

13. −9 ◯ 8
14. 14 ◯ −14
15. −19 ◯ 17
16. 23 ◯ −25

17. −18 ◯ −16
18. 13 ◯ −14
19. 25 ◯ −26
20. 32 ◯ −41

Order each set of integers from least to greatest.

21. 33, −34, 38

_____

22. 9, −17, −13

_____

23. 21, −19, 20, −21

_____

24. 52, −61, 63, −64

_____

Solve.

25. The low temperature on Saturday was −5°F. The low temperature on Sunday was −9°F. Which day was colder?

_____

26. On one play a football team moved the ball −6 yards. On the next play, they moved the ball exactly the opposite. Did they gain or lose yards on the second play? How many yards?

_____

Name _____ Date _____

Reteach

Problem-Solving Strategy

5MR1.1, 5NS2.1

Work Backward

A scientist plans to study exotic birds in the rain forest. The helicopter flight to and from the rain forest costs $499. Supplies cost $112 for each day. How many days can the scientist spend in the rain forest on a $1,283 budget?

Step 1
Understand
	Be sure you understand the problem.
	Read carefully.
	What do you know?
	    • A helicopter flight costs _____.
	    • Supplies cost _____.
	    • The budget is _____.
	What do you need to find?
	    • The _____ in the rain forest.

Step 2 Plan	**Make a plan.** Choose a strategy. You can work backward to find the number of days the scientist can stay in the rain forest. Use math operations to undo each step.
Step 3 Solve	**Carry out your plan.** Decide which operation undoes each step. Undo the addition of the cost of the helicopter. Which operation undoes addition? _____ _____ the cost of the helicopter from the total budget: _____ The scientist has _____ left after paying for the helicopter. Undo the multiplication of the number of days the scientist can stay in the rain forest. Which operation undoes multiplication? _____ _____ the amount remaining by the cost of supplies for each day. _____ days How many days can the scientist stay in the rain forest? _____

7-5

Reteach

5MR1.1, 5NS2.1

Problem-Solving Strategy (continued)

Step 4 Check	**Is the solution reasonable?** Reread the problem. Have you answered the question? _____ How can you check your answer? _____

Solve. Use the *work backward* strategy.

1. Ms. Robin's class is planting trees for Arbor Day. They raise a total of $80 to buy trees and supplies. A local nursery has offered to provide trees for $7 each. They spend $17 on supplies. How many trees do they buy?

   _____

2. Mr. Stone's class visits the aquarium. Mr. Stone has $46 for the trip. The entrance fee for the class is $34. The rest of the money is used to buy posters for the classroom. Each poster costs $3. How many posters does Mr. Stone buy?

   _____

Name _____ Date _____

Skills Practice

Problem-Solving Strategy

5MR1.1, 5NS2.1

Work Backward

Solve. Use the *work backward* strategy.

1. Ms. Houston's fifth grade class is going to a dinosaur park. The class raises $68 for the trip. Transportation to the park costs $40. The park sells small fossils for $4 each. How many fossils can they buy with the money they have left?

_____

2. **Time** Kusuo's baseball game begins at 5:00 P.M. Kusuo wants to arrive 45 minutes early to warm up. If it takes him $\frac{1}{2}$ hour to get to the baseball field, what time should Kusuo leave his home for the game?

_____

Use any strategy to solve.

3. A theater seats 44 people. For Friday evening performances, 128 tickets were sold. How many performances were there on Friday evening?

_____

4. **Science** Many huskies have one brown eye and one blue eye and others have two blue eyes. In a group of 22 huskies, there were 38 blue eyes. How many of the dogs have two blue eyes?

_____

5. **Number Sense** Steffy picks a number, subtracts 13, and then multiplies the difference by 2. Finally, she adds 8 to the product. Her final number is 122. What was her starting number?

_____

6. **Create a problem** for which you could work backward to solve. Share it with others.

_____

Name _____ Date _____

Reteach

5MR2.4, 5NS2.1

Problem-Solving Investigation

Choose the Best Strategy

The high tide at Sunshine Beach on Monday was 7 feet. The low tide on Monday was −3 feet. Molly claimed that the difference in the heights of the tides was 4 feet. Use logical reasoning to find out if Molly's claim is correct.

Step 1 Understand	What do you know? High tide was _____ and low tide was _____ . What do you need to find out? _____
Step 2 Plan	Which operation should you use to find the difference in the heights of the tides? _____ What is Molly's claim? _____ _____
Step 3 Solve	Complete. The difference between a positive integer and a negative integer is always _____ the positive integer. Evaluate Molly's claim. Explain. _____ _____
Step 4 Check	To check, find the difference. _____ The difference was _____.

Use any strategy shown below to solve.

- Use logical reasoning   • Work backward   • Guess and check

1. On Thursday, the high tide reached 4 feet. The low tide on Thursday was 7 feet lower than high tide. Glen calculated that the low tide was 3 feet. Is his calculation correct? Explain.

2. At 2 A.M., the temperature was −3°F. By 6 A.M., the temperature had risen 4°F. Carmen calculates the temperature at 6 A.M. is 1°F. Is her calculation correct? Explain.

3. Your parents have given you twice as many dollars as your age on each birthday since your fifth birthday. If you are 10 years old, how much money have you been given over the years?

_____

4. Find the missing term in the pattern below.

..... _____, 2, 5, 8, 11, 14

_____

5. Sarah needs to arrive at work at 7:45 A.M. It takes her 12 minutes to drive to her office, 15 minutes to make and eat breakfast, and 37 minutes to get ready. What time does she need to set her alarm for to get to work on time?

_____

6. On Wednesday, 72 cookbooks were sold at a book sale. This is 9 more than one half the amount sold on Tuesday. How many cookbooks were sold on Tuesday?

_____

7. Robert has 39 model cars and his brother, Frank, has 56 model cars. How many more model cars does Robert need to have the same number as his brother?

_____

8. The local pet store made a profit if $300 in March, but only made a profit of $150 in April. How much more did the pet store make in March?

_____

Name _____ Date _____

Skills Practice

Problem-Solving Investigation

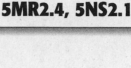

Choose the Best Strategy

Use any strategy shown below to solve.

• Use logical reasoning • Work backward • Guess and check

1. At 3 A.M, the tide was –4 feet. By 9 A.M., the tide had risen 6 feet. Andre calculates that the tide reached 10 feet at 9 A.M. Is his calculation correct? Explain.

2. A scuba diver descended 8 feet below the surface of the water. Then he descended an additional 12 feet. He then ascends 3 feet. Write an integer to show his distance from the surface.

3. A croquet ball has a mass of 460 grams. Together, the mass of a golf ball and a croquet ball is the same as the mass of 11 golf balls. What is the mass of one golf ball?

4. The temperature recorded at 5 A.M. was 25°F. The temperature increased by 2°F for every hour for the next four hours. What was the temperature at the end of the four hours?

Choose the correct answer.

At Clearview Beach, the lowest tide of the year was –9 feet. The highest tide for the year was 12 feet.

5. Which of the following is true?

   A The range in the highest and lowest tides for the year is 21 feet.

   B The tide changes by 3 feet from high tide to low tide.

   C The highest tide for the year reached 21 feet.

   D The lowest tide for the year reached –12 feet.

6. When checking if an answer is reasonable,

   F rework the problem at least three times.

   G compare it with known facts.

   H guess whether or not the answer looks correct.

   J use multiplication to solve.

Name _____ Date _____

Reteach

5AF1.5

Solving Addition Equations

You can use subtraction to solve addition equations.

Solve: $c + 25 = 39$

To find the value of c,
subtract 25 from each side of the equation.

$$
\begin{aligned}
c + 25 &= 39 \\
-25 &= -25 \\
\hline
c &= 14
\end{aligned}
$$

Check your answer by substituting 14 for c
in the original equation.

$$
\begin{aligned}
c + 25 &= 39 \\
14 + 25 &= 39 \\
39 &= 39 \leftarrow \text{It checks.}
\end{aligned}
$$

Solve each equation. Check your solution.

1. $n + 36 = 75$

$-\boxed{}-\boxed{}$

$n = $ _____

2. $b + 4.6 = 15.9$

$-\boxed{}-\boxed{}$

$b = $ _____

3. $w + \dfrac{1}{8} = \dfrac{7}{8}$

$-\boxed{}-\boxed{}$

$w = $ _____

4. $p + 7 = 83$

$p = $ _____

5. $c + 46 = 213$

$c = $ _____

6. $s + 8 = 4$

$s = $ _____

7. $a + 9 = 3$

$a = $ _____

8. $z + 10 = -4$

$z = $ _____

9. $y + 1 = -8$

$y = $ _____

10. $-5 = g + 8$

$g = $ _____

11. $-4 = z + 1$

$z = $ _____

12. $9 = m + 4$

$m = $ _____

7–9

Skills Practice

5AF1.5

Solving Addition Equations

Solve each equation. Check your solution.

1. $a + 8 = 23$ _____

2. $s + 9 = 26$ _____

3. $f + 36 = 58$ _____

4. $z + 6 = -4$ _____

5. $v + 14 = 162$ _____

6. $h + 2.7 = 3.8$ _____

7. $k + 20 = -10$ _____

8. $t + 30 = 94$ _____

9. $r + \frac{3}{4} = 17$ _____

10. $-9 = d + 1$ _____

11. $s + 14.9 = 31.6$ _____

12. $10 = c + 21$ _____

13. $4.5 = e + 0.4$ _____

14. $z + 2\frac{1}{2} = 6\frac{3}{4}$ _____

15. $-52 = g + 30$ _____

16. $c + 200 = 473$ _____

17. $w + 35 = 5$ _____

18. $p + \frac{2}{3} = 7$ _____

Solve.

19. The high temperature one day in Washington, D.C., was 40°F. That was 14°F greater than the low temperature. Write an addition equation to describe the situation. Use *t* to represent the low temperature. Then solve the equation.

_____

_____

20. One year Chicago, IL, received 39.2 inches of snow. That was 9.8 inches more than the previous year. Write an addition equation to describe the situation. Solve it to find last year's snowfall in inches, *s*.

_____

_____

Reteach

Solving Subtraction Equations

You can use addition to solve subtraction equations.

Solve: $f - 2 = 13$

To find the value of f, add 2 to
both sides of the equation.

$$\begin{array}{r} f - 2 = 13 \\ + 2 = + 2 \\ \hline f = 15 \end{array}$$

Check your answer by substituting 15
for f in the original equation.

$$f - 2 = 13$$
$$15 - 2 = 13$$
$$13 = 13 \leftarrow \text{It checks.}$$

Solve each equation. Check your solution.

1. $a - 7 = 10$ _____

2. $j - 3 = 11$ _____

3. $\ell - 9 = 1$ _____

4. $p - 11 = -5$ _____

5. $b - 9 = 6$ _____

6. $g - 10 = -4$ _____

7. $m - 7 = 12$ _____

8. $i - 12 = 2$ _____

9. $d - 2 = 8$ _____

10. $k - 3 = 6$ _____

11. $z - 2 = -11$ _____

12. $r - 7 = -2$ _____

13. $n - 4 = -11$ _____

14. $y - 9 = 1$ _____

15. $f - 2 = 1$ _____

16. $q - 8 = 3$ _____

17. $c - 15 = 5$ _____

18. $h - 4 = -3$ _____

7–10

Skills Practice

5AF1.5

Solving Subtraction Equations

Solve each equation. Check your solution.

1. $n - 4 = 9$ _____

2. $d - 3 = 6$ _____

3. $b - 7 = 3$ _____

4. $r - 4 = 4$ _____

5. $y - 8 = 14$ _____

6. $s - 4 = -2$ _____

7. $9 = d - 6$ _____

8. $m - 7 = 9$ _____

9. $3 = w - 7$ _____

10. $4 = z - 6$ _____

11. $f - 3 = -12$ _____

12. $-2 = t - 1$ _____

13. $a - 10 = 4$ _____

14. $v - 9 = 2$ _____

15. $5 = i - 3$ _____

16. $a - 7 = 2$ _____

17. $v - 10 = -2$ _____

18. $-3 = n - 1$ _____

19. $7 = i - 6$ _____

20. $-7 = r - 4$ _____

Solve.

21. Leah started with d dollars. After Leah spent $19, she had $13 left. Write a subtraction equation to represent this situation. Then solve the equation to find the amount of money Leah started with.

_____

_____

22. A chapter has 45 pages. Larry has read n pages, and has 8 pages left. Write a subtraction equation to represent this situation. Then solve the equation to find the number of pages Larry has left to read.

_____

_____

Name _____ Date _____

Reteach

Solving Multiplication Equations

You can use division to solve multiplication equations.

Solve: $12s = 240$

To find the value of s,
divide both sides of the equation by 12.

$$12s = 240$$
$$\frac{12s}{12} = \frac{240}{12}$$
$$s = 20$$

Check your answer by substituting 20 for s
in the original equation.

$$12s = 240$$
$$12 \times 20 = 240$$
$$240 = 240 \leftarrow \text{It checks.}$$

Solve each equation. Check your solution.

1. $8d = 96$

$d =$ _____

2. $2.5m = 75$

$m =$ _____

3. $\frac{1}{2}k = 3.2$

$k =$ _____

4. $0.7y = 42$

$y =$ _____

5. $15n = 60$

$n =$ _____

6. $7w = 56$

$w =$ _____

7. $\frac{3}{4}a = \frac{1}{2}$

$a =$ _____

8. $9v = 72$

$v =$ _____

9. $30b = 600$

$b =$ _____

10. $2a = 26$

$a =$ _____

11. $5b = -25$

$b =$ _____

12. $-3z = 51$

$z =$ _____

13. $-2x = 10$

$x =$ _____

14. $7y = 49$

$y =$ _____

15. $-3a = -15$

$a =$ _____

16. $3b = 45$

$b =$ _____

17. $8x = -64$

$x =$ _____

18. $-9z = 27$

$z =$ _____

Name _____ Date _____

Skills Practice

Solving Multiplication Equations

Solve each equation. Check your solution.

1. $7w = 28$ _____

2. $6q = 108$ _____

3. $20d = 180$ _____

4. $6a = 12$ _____

5. $4e = 276$ _____

6. $15y = 48$ _____

7. $8k = 40$ _____

8. $0.4p = 16$ _____

9. $3j = 39$ _____

10. $12s = 60$ _____

11. $30h = 15$ _____

12. $8w = 64$ _____

13. $-3y = 12$ _____

14. $2.4c = 120$ _____

15. $10x = -20$ _____

16. $7s = 21$ _____

17. $4x = 12$ _____

18. $32f = 6.4$ _____

19. $0.6t = 60$ _____

20. $-4w = 24$ _____

Solve.

21. The Martinez family paid $37.50 for 5 movie passes. Write a multiplication equation to describe the situation. Solve it to find the cost in dollars, c, of each movie pass.

_____

22. Three friends each bought a gift. Each of the presents cost the same amount. All together, they paid $15. Write a multiplication equation to describe the situation.

_____

Reteach

Ratios and Rates

A **ratio** is used to compare two quantities by division. You can write different ratios to compare these circles and squares in different ways. You can also write each ratio in different ways.

A **rate** is a ratio comparing two quantities with different kinds of units.

4 circles
3 squares
7 total shapes

	Part to Part circles to squares	**Part to Whole** circles to total shapes	**Whole to Part** total shapes to squares
Using the word *to*	4 to 3	4 to 7	7 to 3
Using a colon	4:3	4:7	7:3
As a fraction	$\frac{4}{3}$	$\frac{4}{7}$	$\frac{7}{3}$
In words	four to three	four to seven	seven to three

Write each ratio as a fraction in simplest form.

1. circles : squares

$\dfrac{5}{\boxed{}}$

2. circles to total shapes

$\dfrac{\boxed{}}{\boxed{}}$

Write each rate as a unit rate.

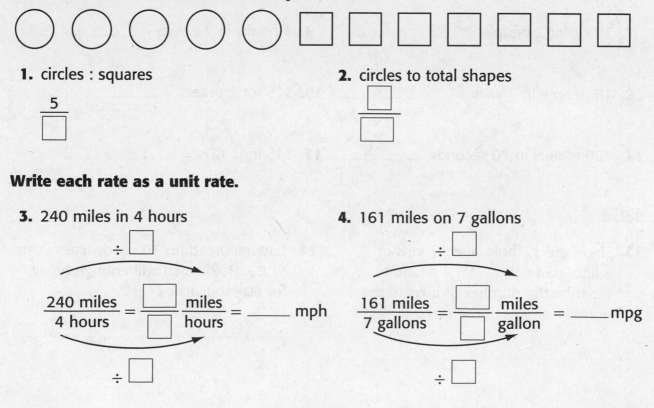

3. 240 miles in 4 hours

$$\frac{240 \text{ miles}}{4 \text{ hours}} = \frac{\boxed{}}{\boxed{}} \frac{\text{miles}}{\text{hours}} = \underline{\quad} \text{ mph}$$

4. 161 miles on 7 gallons

$$\frac{161 \text{ miles}}{7 \text{ gallons}} = \frac{\boxed{}}{\boxed{}} \frac{\text{miles}}{\text{gallon}} = \underline{\quad} \text{ mpg}$$

Name _____ Date _____

Skills Practice

Ratios and Rates

Write each ratio as a fraction in simplest form.

○ ○ ○ ○ ○ ○   ▭▭ ▭▭ ▭▭ ▭

1. circles to rectangles

_____

2. rectangles : circles

_____

3. total : rectangles

_____

4. circles to total

_____

Write each rate as a unit rate.

5. 120 miles in 3 hours = _____

6. 27 pages in 2 days = _____

7. 10 oz for 2 people = _____

8. 3 books in 2 weeks = _____

9. 16 people in 4 vans = _____

10. $15 for 2 tickets = _____

11. 100 meters in 10 seconds _____

12. $45 for 3 CDs = _____

Solve.

13. There are 12 boys and 11 girls in a fifth-grade class. Write a ratio to describe the number of boys to the number of girls in the class.

_____

14. Enough bread for 10 sandwiches costs $1.89. How much will enough bread for 80 sandwiches cost?

_____

Name _____ Date _____

Reteach

5MR1.1, 5NS2.1

Problem-Solving Strategy

Look for a Pattern

A high school student practices the high jump, starting the bar at 3 feet 4 inches and raising the bar 0.5 inch after each jump. How high will the bar be on the fifth jump?

Step 1 Understand	**What facts do you know?**
	• The student starts the bar at _____.
	• The student raises the bar _____ after each jump.
	What do you need to find?
	• You need to find how high _____.
Step 2 Plan	**Make a plan.**
	Using a pattern will help you solve the problem.
	Organize the information in a chart.
Step 3 Solve	**Carry out your plan.**
	Make a chart. Look for a pattern in the chart.

Jump Number	1	2	3	4	5
Bar Height	3 feet 4 inches	3 feet 4.5 inches	3 feet 5 inches	3 feet 5.5 inches	

Look at the chart to find the pattern.

What is the pattern?

_____

Continue the pattern to predict the height for the fifth jump.

Jump 5: 3 feet 5.5 inches + 0.5 inch = _____

Using the pattern, you can expect that the bar will be set at

_____ for the fifth jump.

Name _____ Date _____

Reteach

Problem-Solving Strategy (continued)

Step 4
Check

Is the solution reasonable?

Look back at the problem.

Have you answered the question? _____

Does your answer make sense? _____

Did you find a pattern and continue it? _____

Solve. Use the *look for a pattern* strategy.

1. On the first day of the crafts fair, 200 people show up. Each day thereafter, the number of people who attend the fair increases by 150. The crafts fair runs for five days. How many people attend the fair on the last day?

_____

2. A pole vaulter raises the bar 1 inch after each successful vault. To begin the bar is at 6 feet 3 inches. How high will the bar be after 4 successful vaults?

_____

3. ALGEBRA Find the next three numbers in the pattern below. Then describe the pattern.

−5, 0, 5, 10, ____, ____, ____

_____

4. ALGEBRA Describe the pattern below. Then find the missing number.

10, 20, 30, ____, 50

_____

Name _____ Date _____

Skills Practice
Problem-Solving Strategy

5MR1.1, 5NS2.1

Solve. Use the *look for a pattern* strategy.

1. A student just learning the high jump starts with the bar at 3 feet. The pole is raised 0.25 inch after each successful jump. How high will the bar be after 12 successful jumps?

_____

2. A beginning pole vaulter raises the bar 0.5 inch after each successful vault. On the first jump the bar is at 4 feet 5 inches. How high will the bar be after 3 successful vaults?

_____

3. **ART** A designer is making a tile mosaic. The first row of the mosaic has 1 red tile in the center. If the designer increases the number of red tiles in the center of each row by 4, how many red tiles will be in the center of the fifth row?

_____

4. **HEALTH** Brian has started an exercise program in which he walks daily. He plans to increase the distance that he walks by 0.25 mile each week. He walks 2.25 miles everyday the first week. How many miles will he be walking each day during the fifth week?

_____

Mixed Strategy Review

Use any strategy to solve each problem.

5. **NUMBER SENSE** The sum of two whole numbers between 20 and 40 is 58. The difference of the two numbers is 12. What are the two numbers?

_____

Strategy: _____

6. Ramon has $3.50. He buys two pens that cost $0.75 each and a pencil that costs $0.40. How much money does Ramon have left?

_____

Strategy: _____

167

8–3

Reteach

5MR2.3, 5NS2.1

Ratio Tables

To make one serving of a flavored milk drink, 2 ounces of flavoring is mixed with 1 cup of milk. How many ounces of flavoring and how many cups of milk do you need to mix enough for three servings?

Step 1 Understand the exercise and the amounts identified. It may help to draw a picture of the amounts.	1 serving = 2 ounces of flavoring 1 cup of milk
Step 2 Make a plan to find the information you need.	How much milk and flavoring is needed for 3 servings? Create a ratio table and organize quantities within the columns. The columns of a ratio table are filled with pairs of numbers that have the same ratio. <table><tr><td>**Cups of Milk**</td><td>1</td><td>2</td><td>3</td><td>4</td></tr><tr><td>**Ounces of Flavoring**</td><td>2</td><td>4</td><td>6</td><td>8</td></tr></table> $\frac{1}{2}$, $\frac{2}{4}$, and $\frac{3}{6}$ are equivalent since each simplifies to a ratio of $\frac{1}{2}$.
Step 3 Solve. Find the ratio in simplest form.	One cup is one serving, so three cups are three servings. $\frac{3}{6}$ is the ratio that answers the question. You will need 3 cups of milk and 6 ounces of flavoring. In simplest terms, the ratio is 1:2.
Step 4 Check. Is the solution reasonable? Reread the problem.	Have you answered the question? Does your answer make sense?

Use a ratio table to solve the problem.

1. To make 1 cup of pink icing add 4 drops of red coloring to 1 cup of white icing. How much of each ingredient do you need to make 6 cups of icing that is the same shade of pink?

Name _____ Date _____

Skills Practice

Ratio Tables

Use the ratio tables given to solve each problem.

1. To make applesauce, you need 2 cups of sugar for every 16 apples. Use the ratio table to find out how many cups of sugar you need if you have 4 apples.

Cups of Sugar	2			
Apples	16			4

2. Monte receives an allowance of $20 each month. How much money will he receive by the end of the year?

Allowance	$20		
Months	1		12

3. When Russ rides his bike to school and back home every day for 5 days, he covers 20 miles. At this rate, how many miles will he cover if he rides his bike for 30 days?

Days	5		30
Miles	20		

4. A certain 10-ounce soft drink contains 12 teaspoons of sugar. Use a ratio table to determine how many teaspoons of sugar you consume if you drink 15 ounces of this soft drink.

Ounces of Soft Drink	10		15
Teaspoons of Sugar	12		

5. Sonya purchased 650 beads for $52 to make necklaces. If she needs 50 more beads, how much will she pay if she is charged the same rate?

Beads	650		50
Price	$52		

Name _____ Date _____

Reteach

Equivalent Ratios

Determine if each pair of ratios or rates are equivalent. Explain your reasoning.

Two quantities are equivalent if they have a constant ratio or rate.

$$\frac{10 \text{ sandwiches}}{\$6} = \frac{5 \text{ sandwiches}}{\$3} \text{ and } \frac{20 \text{ sandwiches}}{\$12} = \frac{5 \text{ sandwiches}}{\$3}$$

So, $\dfrac{10 \text{ sandwiches}}{\$6} = \dfrac{20 \text{ sandwiches}}{\$12}$.

1. eating peanut butter and jelly sandwiches once every 5 days; eating 4 peanut butter and jelly sandwiches every 20 days

   _____

   _____

2. 2 white kittens per litter; 10 white kittens per 4 litters

   _____

   _____

3. 1 out of 3 cups of yogurt is strawberry; 4 out of 12 cups of yogurt is strawberry

   _____

   _____

4. 8 hours of work for $60 pay; 40 hours of work for $300

   _____

   _____

5. 166 miles driven on 4 gallons of gas; 322 miles driven on 11 gallons of gas

   _____

   _____

6. 15 prints for $3; 60 prints for $9

   _____

   _____

8-4

Skills Practice

Equivalent Ratios

5AF1.5

Determine if each pair of ratios or rates are equivalent. Explain your reasoning.

1. 3 pairs of pants for $60; 4 pairs of pants for $80

_____

_____

2. 18 bagels for $6; 36 bagels for $15

_____

_____

3. You give 12 rings to 4 of your friends. Suzanne gives 24 rings to 8 of her friends.

_____

_____

4. Angelica reads 3 books per month. She reads 36 books in a year.

_____

_____

5. 75 words typed in 5 minutes; 96 words typed in 6 minutes

_____

_____

_____

8–5

Reteach

Problem-Solving Investigation

Choose the Best Strategy

There are 4 players and 1 coach on a tennis team. How many coaches are needed for 36 tennis players?

Step 1 Understand	**Make sure you understand the problem.** What do you know? _____ What do you need to find out? _____
Step 2 Plan	**Make a plan.** You can use the *make a table* strategy to find the number of coaches.
Step 3 Solve	 $\times 9$ 	Number of Coaches	1	9	 	Number of Players	4	36	 $\times 9$ To complete the table, find a factor to multiply by 1. Since $4 \times 9 = 36$, multiply 1×9. So, 9 coaches are needed.
Step 4 Check	Since $\frac{9}{36} = \frac{1}{4}$, the answer is correct.

Name _____ Date _____

Reteach

Problem-Solving Investigation   (continued)

Use any strategy shown below to solve each problem.

- Act it out
- Look for a pattern
- Make a table

1. Mayumi is driving home from college. She has 510 miles left to go. Her average speed is 52 miles per hour. How long will it take for her to get there?

_____

_____

2. Leo goes on a hot-air balloon ride. The ride covers 70 miles and takes 4 hours. What was the speed of the balloon?

_____

_____

3. The number of goals Dana scored in the first three years of playing hockey are shown. At this rate, how many goals should he expect to score at the end of the fourth year?

Year	Goals
1	3
2	5
3	7
4	

4. For a class project, Javier has to create a flag to represent his class. The flag must have 2 solid horizontal stripes (one white and one blue) with a silver diamond in the center of one of the stripes. There are several possibilities for the flag that Javier can create. Find how many different flags Javier can make with two stripes and one diamond.

_____

_____

5. Kim has to drive a total of 275 miles to visit her grandfather. If she drives 65 miles per hour for the first 160 miles and then 70 miles per hour for the rest of the trip, how long will it take her to make the trip?

_____

6. To train for a race, you plan to run 1 mile the first week and double the number of miles each week for five weeks. How many miles will you run the 5th week?

_____

Name _____ Date _____

Skills Practice

Problem-Solving Investigation

Use any strategy shown below to solve each problem.

- Act it out
- Look for a pattern
- Make a table

1. To train for the bicycle race, Dan plans to ride 10 miles per day the first week, adding 3 miles per week. How many miles will he ride per day the eighth week?

_____

2. A rancher is building a square corral with sides that are 20 feet long. He plans to put a post every 5 feet around the edge of the corral. How many posts will he need?

_____

3. At 5 P.M., the temperature was 3°C. By 8 P.M., the temperature had dropped 6°C. What was the temperature at 8 P.M.?

_____

4. Which is greater for the following data: the mode or the median?
8, 10, 4, 7, 36, 21, 8, 11, 19

_____

5. Write a problem that you can solve using a problem-solving strategy. What strategy would you use to solve the problem? Explain why you chose that strategy.

_____

Name _____ Date _____

Reteach

5NS1.2, 5SDAP1.3

Percents and Fractions

You can think of a percent as the numerator of a fraction with 100 as the denominator.

This grid contains 100 small squares. Each square represents 1%. 76 small squares are shaded.

Percent: 76 parts of 100, or 76%

Fraction: 76 parts of 100, or $\frac{76}{100}$. In simplest form, that's $\frac{19}{25}$.

Write a percent and a fraction to show the shaded part of each grid. For each fraction, use simplest form.

1.

_____ shaded parts

_____ total parts

Percent: _____

Fraction: _____

2.

_____ shaded parts

_____ total parts

Percent _____

Fraction: _____

3.

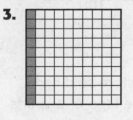

Percent: _____

Fraction: _____

4.

Percent _____

Fraction: _____

Name _____ Date _____

Skills Practice

Percents and Fractions

Write a fraction and a percent to show the shaded part of each grid. For each fraction, use simplest form.

1.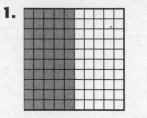

2.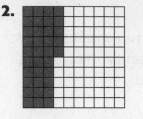

3.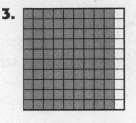

_____   _____   _____

Write each percent as a fraction or mixed number in simplest form.

4. 67% _____   5. 8% _____   6. 243% _____

7. 32% _____   8. 81% _____   9. 148% _____

Write each fraction as a percent.

10. $\frac{1}{4}$ _____   11. $\frac{3}{10}$ _____   12. $\frac{1}{2}$ _____   13. $\frac{40}{100}$ _____

14. $\frac{12}{100}$ _____   15. $\frac{6}{100}$ _____   16. $\frac{23}{100}$ _____   17. $\frac{1}{10}$ _____

18. $\frac{19}{100}$ _____   19. $\frac{99}{100}$ _____   20. $\frac{7}{100}$ _____   21. $\frac{10}{100}$ _____

Solve.

22. Three fourths of the shirts a store stocks are extra large. What percent of the shirts are extra large?

_____

23. Of the 100 shirts a store sold on Saturday, 82 had the logo of a sports team on them. What percent of the shirts had a logo?

_____

9–2

Reteach

Circle Graphs

The table shows the results of a survey of 160 students. You can also display this data in a circle graph. Circle graphs are used to compare parts of a whole.

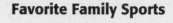

Favorite Family Sport	
Sport	**Percent of Total Responses**
Cycling	25%
Bowling	40%
In-line skating	35%

- Write a fraction for each percent.

  Cycling: $25\% = \dfrac{25}{100}$ or $\dfrac{1}{4}$

  Bowling: $40\% = \dfrac{40}{100}$ or $\dfrac{2}{5}$

  In-line skating: $35\% = \dfrac{35}{100}$ or $\dfrac{7}{20}$

- Since $25\% = \dfrac{1}{4}$, shade $\dfrac{1}{4}$ of the circle for "Cycling." Since 40% is a little less than 50% or $\dfrac{1}{2}$, shade a little less than $\dfrac{1}{2}$ of the circle for "Bowling." The remaining section is for "In-line skating."

- Label each section of the graph.

Favorite Family Sports

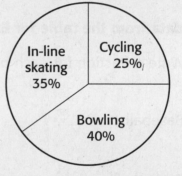

---

1. Sketch a circle graph for the data from the table at the right.

Favorite Team Sport	
Sport	**Percent of Responses**
Basketball	60%
Baseball	25%
Soccer	15%

9–2

Skills Practice

Circle Graphs

5SDAP1.2, 5SDAP1.3

Use data from the circle graph for Exercises 1 and 2.

1. List the activities from favorite to least favorite.

   _____

2. What fraction of the total votes went to in-line skating?

   _____

Favorite After-School Activity

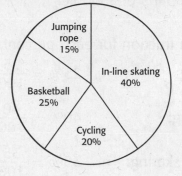

Use data from the table for Exercises 3–4.

3. Write a fraction for each percent.

   Baseball: _____

   Basketball: _____

   Football: _____

   Soccer: _____

Favorite Spectator Sport	
Sport	**Percent of Total Responses**
Baseball	35%
Basketball	30%
Football	15%
Soccer	20%

4. Make a circle graph at the right to show the data.

186

Name _____ Date _____

Reteach

Percents and Decimals

Chapter Resources

You can write percents as decimals.

First, write 35% as a fraction with a denominator of 100.

$$35\% = \frac{35}{100}$$

Then, read the fraction and write the decimal.

$$\frac{35}{100} = 35 \text{ hundredths} = 0.35$$

So, 35% = 0.35.

You can also write decimals as percents.

Write 0.64 as a fraction.

$$0.64 = 64 \text{ hundredths} = \frac{64}{100}$$

Then, write the numerator of the fraction with a percent sign.

$$\frac{64}{100} = 64\%$$

So, 0.64 = 64%.

Write the percent as a decimal.

1. $25\% = \dfrac{\square}{100} =$ _____

2. $40\% = \dfrac{\square}{100} =$ _____

3. $56\% = \dfrac{\square}{100} =$ _____

4. $70\% = \dfrac{\square}{100} =$ _____

5. $93\% = \dfrac{\square}{100} =$ _____

6. $3\% = \dfrac{\square}{100} =$ _____

Write the decimal as a percent.

7. $0.25 = \dfrac{\square}{100} =$ _____

8. $0.9 = \dfrac{\square}{100} =$ _____

9. $0.55 = \dfrac{\square}{100} =$ _____

10. $0.95 = \dfrac{\square}{100} =$ _____

11. $0.51 = \dfrac{\square}{100} =$ _____

12. $0.04 = \dfrac{\square}{100} =$ _____

Name _____ Date _____

Skills Practice

Percents and Decimals

Write each percent as a decimal.

1. 34% _____   **2.** 70% _____   **3.** 48% _____

4. 25% _____   **5.** 7% _____   **6.** 45% _____

7. 12% _____   **8.** 54% _____   **9.** 91% _____

10. 95% _____   **11.** 32% _____   **12.** 82% _____

13. 157% _____ **14.** 24% _____   **15.** 30% _____

16. 18% _____   **17.** 72% _____   **18.** 188% _____

19. 60% _____   **20.** 122% _____ **21.** 96% _____

Write each decimal as a percent.

22. 0.75 _____ **23.** 0.4 _____ **24.** 0.5 _____ **25.** 1.28 _____

26. 1.22 _____ **27.** 0.10 _____ **28.** 0.85 _____ **29.** 0.6 _____

30. 0.75 _____ **31.** 0.2 _____ **32.** 0.88 _____ **33.** 0.03 _____

Find each missing number.

34. $29\% = \dfrac{s}{100}$ **35.** $80\% = \dfrac{w}{5}$ **36.** $44\% = \dfrac{c}{25}$ **37.** $90\% = \dfrac{a}{10}$

$s =$ _____ $w =$ _____ $c =$ _____ $a =$ _____

Name _____ Date _____

Reteach

Problem-Solving Strategy

Solve a simpler problem.

Last year, Jeff made 70% of his attempted free throws in basketball. If he attempted 70 free throws, how many did he make?

Step 1 Understand	**Be sure you understand the problem.** What do you know? You know the percent of free throws that Jeff made last year. You also know the number of free throws he attempted. What do you need to find? You need to find the number of free throws Jeff made.
Step 2 Plan	**Make a plan.** Solve a simpler problem by finding 10% of Jeff's attempted free throws. Use the result to find 70% of his attempted free throws.
Step 3 Solve	**Carry out your plan.** Since 10% = $\frac{10}{100}$ or $\frac{1}{10}$, 10% of Jeff's attempted free throws is 70 ÷ 10, which is 7. Since there are seven groups of 10% in 70%, multiply 7 by 7. So, Jeff made 49 free throws.
Step 4 Check	**Check your answer.** You know that 30% + 70% = 100%. Find 30% of 70, and add it to 49 to see if the total is 70. To find three groups of 10%, multiply 3 by 7 = 21. 21 + 49 = 70.

Solve. Use the *solve a simpler problem* strategy.

1. Eight chefs can cook 40 meals in 3 hours. How many meals can 25 chefs cook in 6 hours?

   _____

2. An airplane flies at a speed of 500 miles per hour. If a train travels at 25% of that speed, how much faster does the plane travel than the train?

   _____

3. Carla's alarm rings every 20 minutes for one hour each morning. How many times does it ring each week?

_____

4. Your brother has $60. He offers you either 40% or three-sixths of it. What amount should you take if you want to get the most money?

_____

5. Ricky polled his classmates and found that 40% of them named spinach as their favorite vegetable. 30/100 of the class liked broccoli best and 1 out of 10 liked carrots best. Which vegetable does most of Ricky's classmates prefer?

_____

6. There are a total of 500 students at Mary's elementary school. Of that total, 40% of the students have a sibling who also attends the school. How many students have siblings at the school?

_____

7. At the pancake breakfast at Jenny's school, 250 people attended. Of those 250 people, 60% were students. How many students attended?

_____

8. Jeremy can cut two lawns in 2 hours. If Jeremy and his friend Nate work at the same speed, how many lawns can they cut in 5 hours?

_____

Name _____ Date _____

Skills Practice

5MR2.2, 5NS1.2

Problem-Solving Strategy

Solve. Use the *solve a simpler problem* strategy.

1. Monica plays forward on her soccer team. Last year, 30% of her shots scored goals. This year, she made 16 goals out of 40. Did Monica improve her record this year? Explain.

   _____

   _____

2. Brian plays tournament table tennis. Last year, he won 72 percent of his games. This year, he has won 15 of his 20 games. Has Brian improved his record? Explain.

   _____

   _____

3. Jessica swims on a swim team. Last year, she placed first 12 times out of 20 in the breaststroke. This year, she has placed first 55 percent of the time. Was Jessica's record of winning better last year or this year? Explain.

   _____

   _____

4. Peter's class takes timed division tests. Last month, Peter completed 66 percent of the problems correctly. This month, he has completed 60 out of 80 problems correctly. Has Peter improved his score? Explain.

   _____

   _____

Name _____ Date _____

Reteach

5MR2.2, 5NS2.5

Estimating with Percents

When you estimate the percent of a number, you are solving a simpler problem.

Estimate the percent of a number.

Estimate 48% of 197.

48% is close to 50% or $\frac{1}{2}$. Round 197 to 200.

$\frac{1}{2}$ of 200 is 100. $\frac{1}{2}$ or *half* means to divide by 2.

So, 48% of 197 is about 100.

Check your answer by using the related multiplication fact.

$100 \times 2 = 200$, which is correct!

Estimate each percent.

1. 22% of 98 _____

2. 46% of 257 _____

3. 18% of 192 _____

4. 67% of 99 _____

5. 29% of 208 _____

6. 79% of 305 _____

Estimate the percent that is shaded.

7.

8.

9. You buy a shirt that is priced at $25. It is on sale for 25% off. About how much money will you save?

_____

Name _____ Date _____

Skills Practice

5MR2.2, 5NS2.5

Estimating with Percents

Estimate each percent.

1. 29% of 190 _____

2. 18% of 48 _____

3. 87% of 155 _____

4. 44% of 205 _____

5. 74% of 99 _____

6. 52% of 295 _____

7. 38% of 248 _____

Estimate the percent that is shaded.

8.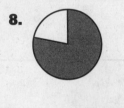

_____

9.

_____

10. You answered 4 out of 25 problems incorrectly on a test. Estimate your percentage of correct answers.

_____

11. If you see a sweatshirt on sale for 15% off, and the sweater is $19.99, estimate the discount.

_____

Name _____ Date _____

Reteach

Percent of a Number

To find the percent of a number, write the percent as a fraction or decimal and multiply. Remember, "of" means "times."

Find 40% of 20.

$40\% = \dfrac{40}{100} = \dfrac{2}{5}$

$\dfrac{2}{5} \times 20 = 8$

40% of 20 = 8

Find 60% of $9.00.

$60\% = \dfrac{60}{100} = 0.60$, or 0.6

$0.6 \times \$9.00 = \$5.40$

60% of $9.00 = $5.40

Find 140% of 20.

$140\% = \dfrac{140}{100} = \dfrac{7}{5}$

$\dfrac{7}{5} \times 20 = 28$

140% of 20 = 28

Find 160% of $9.00

$160\% = \dfrac{160}{100} = 1\dfrac{60}{100} = 1.60$, or 1.6

$1.6 \times \$9.00 = \$14.40$

160% of $9.00 = $14.40

Find the percent of each number.

1. 25% of 24

25% = _____ = _____

_____ × 24 = _____

2. 150% of 38

150% = _____ = _____

_____ × 38 = _____

3. 50% of $8.00

50% = _____ = _____

0. _____ × $8.00 = _____

4. 120% of $20.00

120% = _____ = _____

_____ × $20.00 = _____

5. 140% of 40 _____

6. 80% of $14.00 _____

Name _____ Date _____

Skills Practice

Percent of a Number

Find the percent of each number.

1. 25% of 48 _____

2. 30% of 50 _____

3. 10% of 50 _____

4. 45% of 40 _____

5. 50% of 64 _____

6. 20% of 85 _____

7. 40% of 60 _____

8. 95% of 80 _____

9. 65% of 60 _____

10. 120% of 50 _____

11. 150% of 64 _____

12. 125% of 60 _____

13. 190% of 70 _____

14. 140% of $8 _____

15. 120% of $7 _____

16. 180% of $5 _____

17. 225% of 84 _____

18. 55% of $7 _____

19. 10% of 90 _____

20. 20% of 10 _____

21. 20% of 60 _____

Solve.

22. A football team wins 80% of the 10 games it played. A basketball team wins 45% of 20 games. Which team has won more games? Explain.

_____

Name _____ Date _____

Reteach

Problem-Solving Investigation

5MR1.1, 5NS1.2

Choose a Strategy

Philip and his family caught a lot of fish over a one-week period when they were on vacation.

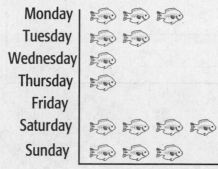

Monday
Tuesday
Wednesday
Thursday
Friday
Saturday
Sunday

Number of Fish Caught

Philip fished on Monday, Wednesday, Friday, and Saturday. His sister, Nancy, fished on Tuesday, Thursday, Friday, and Sunday. What percent of the total fish Philip caught did he catch on Saturday?

Step 1 Understand	**Be sure you understand the problem.** Philip fished on Monday, Wednesday, Friday, and Saturday. Nancy fished on Tuesday, Thursday, Friday, and Sunday.
Step 2 Plan • Work backward. • Look for a pattern. • Solve a simpler problem.	**Make a plan.** Choose a strategy. You can use a four-step plan. Decide what facts you know. Plan what you will do and in what order. Use your plan to solve the problem. Then check your solution to make sure it makes sense.
Step 3 Solve	**Carry out your plan.** Count the number of fish Philip caught. Philip caught $3 + 1 + 0 + 4 = 8$ On Saturday, Philip caught 4 fish. To find the percent, divide 4 by 8. $4 \div 8 = 0.5$ or 5% Philip caught 50% of his fish on Saturday.

Name _____ Date _____

Reteach

Problem-Solving Investigation (continued)

Step 4 Check	**Is the solution reasonable?** Reread the problem. How can you check your answers? _____ _____

Use any strategy shown below to solve.

• Look for a pattern.   • Work backward.   • Solve a simpler problem.

1. Aisha read 24 books over the summer. Jamil read half that many. Taye read twice as many as Aisha. Zina read three times as many as Jamil. Shawon read a third of the number of books that Zina read. Which two students read the same number of books?

   _____

2. Hugo spent some money on school supplies. He received $5 back from the cashier. If he spent $95, how much money did he give the cashier?

   _____

Name _____ Date _____

Skills Practice

Problem-Solving Investigation

Choose the Best Strategy

Use any strategy shown below to solve.

- Look for a pattern.   • Work backward.   • Solve a simpler problem.

1. Digna packed up 10 dinners to deliver from the food shelter. Isabel packed twice as many dinners as Digna. Rosa packed up $\frac{1}{4}$ the amount of meals as Isabel. Juanita packed up three times as many dinners as Rosa. How many dinners in all did the girls prepare? Who prepared the most dinners? Who prepared the least number of dinners?

_____

_____

2. Refer back to question number 1. If it takes the girls 1 hour to deliver 5 meals, in how many hours will they deliver all of the meals? If they break up into two groups, with 2 girls in each group and work at the same rate, how long will it take them to deliver the meals?

_____

3. The Perez family matches the amount of money each of their children puts into their own savings account by 50%. If Luisa put $40 a week into her savings account, how much will she have saved up at the end of the month?

_____

4. Keshia bought a new outfit. She chooses a top that cost $48.95 and leather boots that were twice as much as the top. The pants were one third of the price of the boots. If she received $20.52 back in change, how much money did she give to the cashier?

_____

Name _____ Date _____

Reteach

Probability

6SDAP3.3

If you were to spin this spinner, it could land on A, B, or C. A, B, and C are the possible **outcomes**.

$$P(\text{event}) = \frac{\text{number of favorable outcomes}}{\text{number of possible outcomes}}$$

$P(A) = \dfrac{4}{7}$ ← There are 4 regions marked "A".
         ← There are 7 regions.

Remember to simplify fractions when necessary.

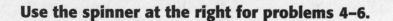

Use the spinner at the right for problems 1–3.

1. $P(X) =$ _____

2. $P(Z) =$ _____

3. $P(X \text{ or } Z) =$ _____

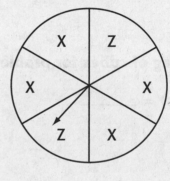

Use the spinner at the right for problems 4–6.

4. $P(P) =$ _____

5. $P(Q) =$ _____

6. $P(P \text{ or } R) =$ _____

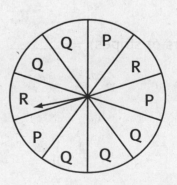

Name _____ Date _____

Skills Practice

6SDAP3.3

Probability

Use the spinner for problems 1–3.

1. *P*(striped) = _____

2. *P*(speckled) = _____

3. *P*(speckled or white) = _____

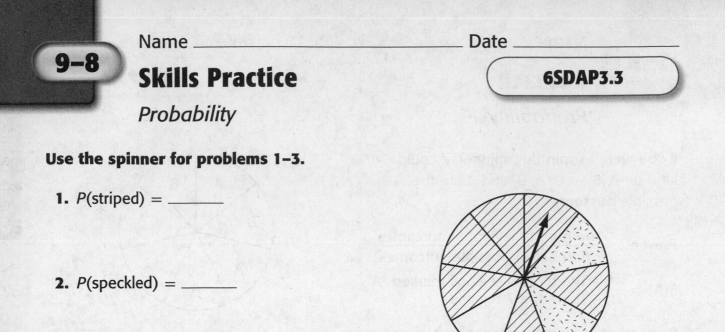

Use the bag of cubes for problems 4–6.

4. *P*(dots) = _____

5. *P*(*not* stripes) = _____

6. *P*(stars or stripes) = _____

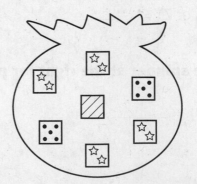

Name _____ Date _____

Reteach

6SDAP3.1

Sample Spaces

The set of all possible outcomes is called a sample space. There are several ways to find the sample space of different situations.

Use a List to Find Sample Space

At the fair you decide to go on the bumper cars, the carousel, and the roller coaster. List all the different orders that you can go on each ride, one time each.

Make an organized list. Use B for bumper cars, C for carousel, and R for roller coaster. Use each letter exactly once.

BCR   BRC   CBR   CRB   RBC   RCB

So there are 6 different orders you can go on each of the rides.

Use a Tree Diagram to Find Probability

Use a tree diagram to find how many pizzas are possible from a choice of thin or thick pizza crust and a choice of pepperoni, mushrooms, or green peppers.

List each crust type. Then pair each crust choice with each topping choice.

Crust	Topping	Outcome
thin crust (N)	pepperoni (P)	NP
	mushrooms (M)	NM
	green pepper (G)	NG
thick crust (K)	pepperoni (P)	KP
	mushrooms (M)	KM
	green pepper (G)	KG

There are six possible pizzas.

Make an organized list or draw a tree diagram to show the sample space for each situation.

1. How many sandwich and fruit combinations can be made if you can choose from a turkey sandwich or ham sandwich with an apple, orange, or banana?

2. In how many ways can Kelly read 4 books, assuming she reads each book once?

Name _____ Date _____

Skills Practice

6SDAP3.1

Sample Spaces

Make an organized list or tree diagram to show the sample space.

1. How many choices do you have for your lunch if you pick either an orange or apple and pretzels or carrots to go with your sandwich?

_____

2. You have a friend over to play. You decide to play cards, have a snack, and then watch a movie. How many different ways can you complete your choices?

_____

3. You are getting ready for school and you only have a choice of a white, purple, or blue shirt and either a pair of jeans, shorts, or a skirt. How many possible outfits can you have?

_____

For the following exercises, toss a number cube and spin the spinner shown.

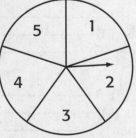

4. Find the number of possible outcomes.   5. Find the *P*(4, less than 3).

_____   _____

6. What is *P*(1, 3)?   7. *P*(even, less than 5)

_____   _____

Name _____ Date _____

Reteach

Making Predictions

> A **survey** is a method of collecting information. The group being surveyed is the population. To save time and money, part of the group, called a **sample**, is surveyed. A good sample is:
> - selected at random, or without preference,
> - representative of the population, and
> - large enough to provide accurate data.

Every sixth student who walked into the school was asked how he or she got to school.

1. What is the probability that a student at the school rode a bike to school?

$$P(\text{ride bike}) = \frac{\text{number of students who rode a bike}}{\text{number of students surveyed}}$$

$$= \frac{10}{40} \text{ or } \frac{1}{4}$$

So, $P(\text{ride bike}) = \frac{1}{4}$, 0.25, or 25%.

School Transportation	
Method	**Students**
walk	10
ride bike	10
ride bus	15
get ride	5

2. There are 360 students at the school. Predict how many bike to school.

Write equivalent ratios. Let s = number of students who will ride a bike.

$$\frac{10}{40} = \frac{s}{360}$$

Since $s = 90$, 90 students will ride a bike to school.

Use the following information and the table shown. Every tenth student entering the school was asked which one of the four subjects was his or her favorite.

1. Find the probability that any student attending school prefers science.

_____

2. There are 400 students at the school. Predict how many students would prefer science.

_____

Favorite Subject	
Subject	**Students**
Language Arts	10
Math	10
Science	15
Social Studies	5

Name _____ Date _____

Skills Practice

Making Predictions

For Exercises 1–2, use the following information.

250 people were asked to name their favorite vacation spot.

1. Find the probability that a person chose an amusement park.

   _____

2. What is the probability that the next person will choose the beach?

   _____

Favorite Vacation Spots	
Beach	150
Amusement Park	70
Campground	30

For Exercises 3–4, use the following information.

Shoppers at a grocery store are asked whether or not they own a pet.

3. How many people were surveyed?

   _____

4. What is the probability that a person owns a pet?

   _____

Do you Own A Pet?	
Yes	52
No	48

For Exercises 5–8, use the table and the following information. A survey of students' favorite sports was taken from a random sample of students in a school. The results are shown in the table.

Students' Favorite Sports	
Soccer	8
Baseball/Softball	3
Volleyball	5
Track & Field	4

5. What is the size of the sample?

   _____

6. There are 550 students in the school. Predict how many students at the school prefer track and field.

   _____

7. What is the probability that a student will prefer volleyball?

   _____

8. What is the probability that a student will prefer soccer?

   _____

Name _____ Date _____

Reteach

5MG2.1

Measuring Angles

You can use a protractor to find the measure of angles.

Measure ∠FGH.

STEP 1 Place the hole of the protractor on the vertex of the angle.

STEP 2 Line up the 0° mark with one side of the angle.

STEP 3 Find where the other side of the angle passes through the same scale. Read the measure of the angle.

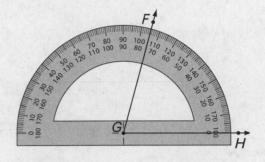

The measure of ∠FGH is 75°.

Use a protractor to find the measure of each angle.

1.

2.

3.

4.

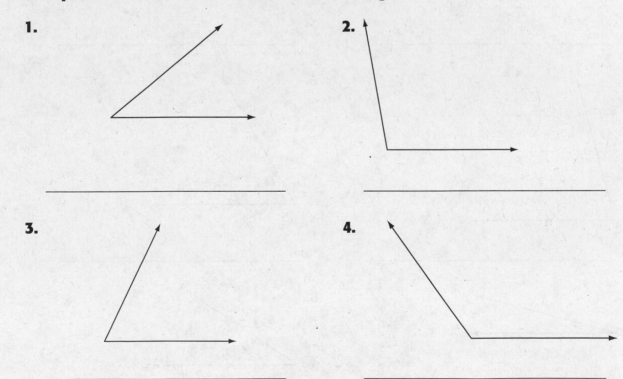

Skills Practice

Measuring Angles

Use a protractor to find the measure of each angle. Then classify
each angle as *acute*, *obtuse*, *right*, or *straight*.

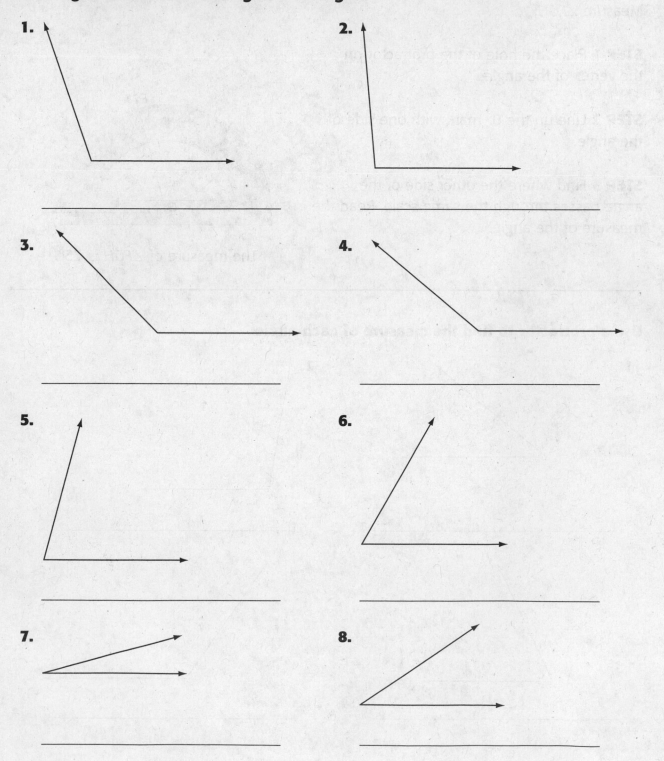

1.

2.

3.

4.

5.

6.

7.

8.

Name _____ Date _____

Reteach

Problem-Solving Strategy

Draw a Diagram

Mark nails a square piece of wood to a wall. The wood measures 35 centimeters on each side. Mark puts a nail every 7 centimeters, including the corners. How many nails does Mark use?

Step 1
Understand
	Be sure you understand the problem.
	
	Read carefully.
	
	What do you know?
	
	   • The piece of wood is a _____ shape.
	
	   • Each side of the square is _____ cm.
	
	   • The nails are _____ apart.
	
	What do you need to find?
	
	   • The _____ Mark uses.

Step 2 Plan	**Make a plan.** Drawing a diagram will help you solve the problem. You can draw a square on graph paper. Label the length of each side of the square. Draw and label dots to represent the nails every 7 centimeters. Then you can count the number of dots on the drawing to find the number of nails Mark uses.

10–2

Reteach

5MR2.3, 5MG2.1

Problem-Solving Strategy (continued)

Step 3 Solve	**Carry out your plan.** Draw a diagram. The piece of wood is square, so you should draw a _____. After you draw the diagram, place _____ at the 4 corners of the square. Then, draw a dot for every _____ on the diagram. Keep in mind the length of each side of the square as you draw in each dot. Use the grid to draw a diagram. To find the number of nails Mark uses, _____ on the diagram. How many nails does Mark use? _____
Step 4 Check	**Is the solution reasonable?** Reread the problem. Have you answered the question? _____ How can you check that your answer is reasonable? _____ _____

Solve. Use the *draw a diagram* strategy.

1. A table 6 feet wide and 8 feet long is set so that there is a plate every 2 feet, except at the corners. How many plates are on the table?

   _____

2. To enclose a garden that is 15 feet long and 12 feet wide, fence posts are set every 3 feet, including the corners. How many posts are needed to enclose the yard?

   _____

Name _____ Date _____

Skills Practice

Problem-Solving Strategy

5MR2.3, 5MG2.1

Chapter Resources

Solve. Use the *draw a diagram* strategy.

1. For a concert, Ron must set the speakers for a sound system every 10 yards around the walls of a square room. Speakers are not set up in the corners of the room. The room is 60 yards long. How many speakers will Ron set up?

   _____

2. Katya makes a 4-by-4 grid. She writes the numbers 0 through 15 in order on the grid, starting with the top left square; moving from left to right along each row. What are the four numbers in the right column of the grid?

   _____

3. Pine cones are evenly spaced on a circular wreath. The third pine cone is opposite the ninth pine cone. How many pine cones are on the wreath?

   _____

4. Jason is building a dog run that is 24 feet by 18 feet. He is setting a fence post every 6 feet and one at each corner. How many posts will he need in all?

   _____

Solve. Use any strategy.

5. Tami, Evan, and Scott each prefer a different type of music. They listen to rock, rap, and country. Tami does not like country. Evan does not like country or rap. Which type of music does each person like best?

   _____

   Strategy: _____

6. The writer F. Scott Fitzgerald was born in St. Paul, Minnesota in 1896. The city of his birth was first called Pig's Eye when it was established 56 years earlier. The name of the city was changed to St. Paul one year after it was established. What year was the city named St. Paul?

   _____

   Strategy: _____

10-3

Reteach

Estimating and Drawing Angles

To estimate the measure of an angle, use measures you know, such as 45°, 90°, and 180°. You can estimate the angle to be a bit smaller or larger than these measures.

a   *b*

Estimate the measurements of these angles. Angle *a* is a little larger than 90°. So, a good estimate is 93°. What about angle *b*? What measurement is it closest to? Circle the best answer.

     45°   90°   180°

Is it *smaller* or *larger* than this measurement? Circle the best answer.

    smaller larger

What is a good estimate for angle *b*? _____

Estimate the measure of each angle.

1.

_____

2.

_____

3.

_____

10–3

Skills Practice

Estimating and Drawing Angles

Estimate the measure of each angle.

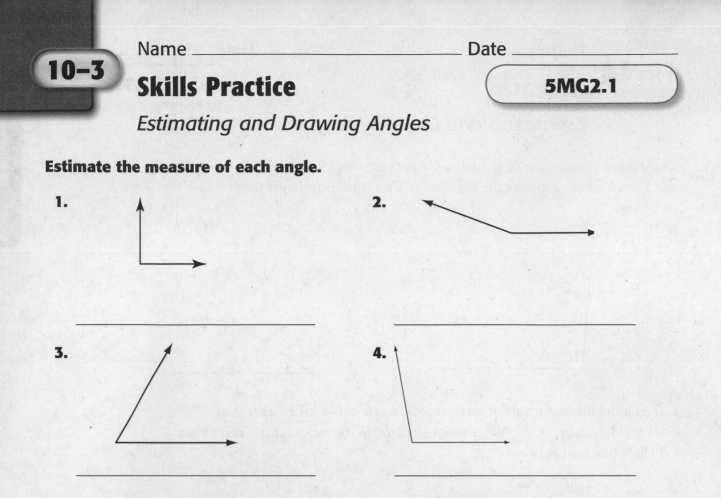

1.

2.

_____

3.

4.

_____

Use a protractor and a straightedge to draw angles having the following measurements.

5. 125°   **6.** 50°   **7.** 80°

_____   _____   _____

8. Look at the letter A. Estimate the measure of the angle inside the top of the letter.

_____

9. Estimate the measure of the angle between the straight back of a chair and the floor.

_____

Name _____ Date _____

Reteach

Problem-Solving Investigation

5MR1.1, 5MG2.1

Choose the Best Strategy

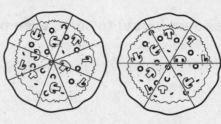

Which part of the pizza is larger, $\frac{3}{8}$ of the first pizza or $\frac{2}{6}$ of the second pizza?

Step 1 Understand	Be sure you understand the problem. You need to compare the two parts of the pizzas, and find which one is larger.
Step 2 Plan • Look for a pattern • Draw a diagram • Guess and check	Make a plan. Choose a strategy. You already have a diagram of the two pizzas. You can also use the four-step plan. Decide what facts you know. Plan what you will do and in what order. Use your plan to solve the problem. Then check your solution to make sure it makes sense.
Step 3 Solve	Carry out your plan. The pizza parts are close in size, so change each fraction to a decimal in order to compare the sizes accurately. $\frac{3}{8}$ and $\frac{2}{6}$ can both be changed into a decimal by dividing. $3 \div 8 = 0.375$ and $2 \div 6 \approx 0.333$ Compare 0.375 to 0.333. Which is larger? 0.375, or $\frac{3}{8}$.
Step 4 Check	Is the solution reasonable? Reread the problem. How can you check your answer? _____ _____

10–5

Reteach

5MR1.1, 5MG2.1

Problem-Solving Investigation   (continued)

Use any strategy shown below to solve each problem.

- Look for a pattern
- Draw a diagram
- Guess and check

1. Which is more, $\frac{7}{8}$ of an apple pie or $\frac{8}{9}$ of the same pie?

_____

2. On Monday, Veronica had 20 minutes of homework. On Tuesday, she had 30 minutes, and on Wednesday, she had 40 minutes. If the pattern continues, how much homework will she have on Friday?

_____

3. Charo is three times as old as Lorena. In 5 years, Lorena will be half Charo's age. How old are Lorena and Charo now?

_____

4. Justin has 6 shirts and 5 pairs of pants. If he wears a different combination each day, how many days will pass before he has to repeat a combination?

_____

5. An artist drew a circle, two lines, and a triangle. What shape will the artist draw next?

_____

6. At a party, everyone shook hands with everyone else exactly once. There were a total of 28 handshakes in the room. How many people were at the party?

_____

10–5

Skills Practice

Problem-Solving Investigation

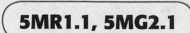

Use any strategy shown below to solve each problem.

- Look for a pattern
- Draw a diagram
- Guess and check

Use the picture to answer Exercises 1 and 2.

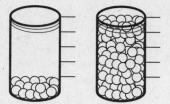

1. Suppose there are 125 marbles in the jar on the right and 25 marbles in the jar on the left. Write a fraction to show the empty part of the first container.

   _____

2. What is the difference between the amounts in each container?

   _____

3. In 2006 you sold 25 rolls of wrapping paper for a fundraiser. In 2007 you sold 30 rolls. If the trend continues, how many rolls will you sell in 2008?

   _____

4. Look at the pattern below. What are the next three bugs?
   Ladybug, ladybug, bee, ant, ladybug, ladybug, bee, ant, ladybug

   _____

Name _____ Date _____

Reteach

5MG2.1, 5MG2.2

Quadrilaterals

You can classify quadrilaterals by their sides and angles.

parallelogram

opposite sides congruent

opposite sides parallel

rectangle

opposite sides congruent

opposite sides parallel

4 right angles

square

all sides congruent

opposite sides parallel

4 right angles

rhombus

all sides congruent, opposite sides parallel

trapezoid

exactly one pair of parallel sides

Circle the characteristics of each quadrilateral. Then classify the quadrilateral in as many ways as possible.

1.

opposite sides congruent

all sides congruent

opposite sides parallel

exactly one pair of parallel sides

4 right angles

_____

2.

opposite sides congruent

all sides congruent

opposite sides parallel

exactly one pair of parallel sides

4 right angles

_____

Name _____ Date _____

Skills Practice

Quadrilaterals

Classify each quadrilateral.

1.

_____

2.

_____

3.

_____

Determine whether each statement is *sometimes*, *always*, or *never* true. Explain your reasoning.

4. A square is a rhombus.

_____

_____

5. A trapezoid has exactly one pair of congruent sides.

_____

_____

6. A rhombus is a parallelogram.

_____

_____

Solve.

7. Lee drew a quadrilateral with three angles that measure 120 degrees, 110 degrees, and 70 degrees. What is the measure of the fourth angle?

_____

8. Robert drew a parallelogram with two 55-degree angles. What are the measures of the other two angles?

_____

Name _____ Date _____

Reteach

Drawing Three-Dimensional Figures

Look at the figure.

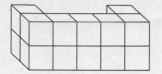

Can you draw the top, front, and side view of this figure?

Pretend you are a bird flying over the figure. What would you see? This is the *top view*. It should be flat, or two-dimensional.

Now pretend you saw the figure from the side. Draw the *side view*.

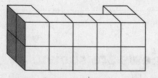

Lastly, shade the front of the figure. Then draw the *front view*.

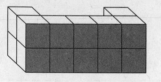

Draw a top, a side, and a front view of each figure.

1.

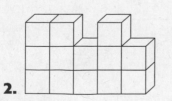

2.

Name _____ Date _____

Skills

5MG2.3

Drawing Three-Dimensional Figures

Draw a top, a side, and a front view of each prism.

1.

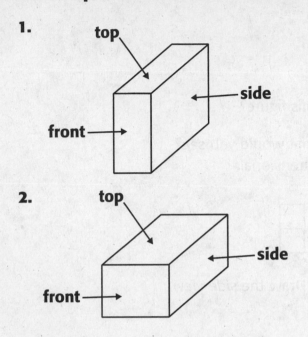

2.

_____

Draw the three-dimensional figure whose top, side, and front views are shown. Use isometric dot paper.

3.

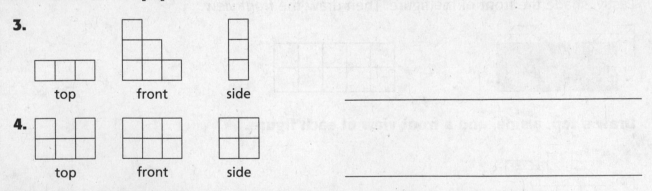

top   front   side

_____

4.

top   front   side

_____

Determine whether each statement is *always*, *sometimes*, or *never* true. Explain your reasoning.

5. You can draw the top, side, and front view of a two-dimensional figure.

_____

6. The top view of a pyramid is a square.

_____

Name _____ Date _____

Reteach

Problem-Solving Strategy

Make a Model

Solve. Use the *make a model* strategy.

Pedro is laying out tiles for a design in his bathroom. The area is 20 inches by 16 inches, and the tiles are 2-inch squares. How many square tiles are needed to fill the area?

Step 1 Understand	**Be sure you understand the problem.** Pedro is laying 2-inch tile in a 20-inch by 16-inch area.
Step 2 Plan Make a model using paper to find the number of tiles needed.	**Make a plan.** You can use a piece of construction paper and small square pieces of paper to represent the tiles.
Step 3 Solve	**Carry out your plan.** Make a model of the area by measuring out a 20″ × 16″ rectangle on construction paper. 20 in. 16 in. Cut out 2-inch squares from another piece of paper. Cover the 20″ × 16″ area completely with the squares. It will take 80 squares or tiles.
Step 4 Check	**Is the solution reasonable?** Reread the problem. Calculate to check your answer. Find the area of 20″ × 16″. It is 320 sq in. Each 2 inch tile has an area of 2″ × 2″ = 4 sq in. 320 sq in. ÷ 4 sq in. = 80 tiles

Name _____ Date _____

Reteach

Problem-Solving Strategy (continued)

Solve. Use the *make a model* strategy.

1. Hugo is making a block tower. Each block is a 4-inch square and is 1 inch thick. If he has 35 blocks, what is the tallest height he can make with the blocks?

   _____

2. Susan wants to organize her bookcase in her bedroom. It consists of 3 shelves and each shelf is 36 inches long. If she has 25 two-inch wide books, 15 three-inch wide books, and 32 one-inch wide books, will she be able to fit them on the three shelves? If not, how many of each book will not fit?

   _____

   _____

3. Patricia is making a clay game board. Each square needs to be 2 inches. If the square board will be 16 inches on each side, how many total squares will it have?

   _____

4. Pablo has a sheet of stickers that is 11 inches long. Each sticker is a square with a side length of 1 inch. There are 10 stickers in each row. There is no space between stickers. How many stickers are there on one page?

   _____

5. Charo is making a picture frame with shells she found. Each shell is 2 inches long. If she makes a rectangular frame out of 20 shells, how large can she make the frame?

   _____

Name _____ Date _____

Skills Practice

Problem-Solving Strategy

Solve. Use the *make a model* strategy.

1. Ping and Kuri are designing a small end table using 1-inch tiles. If Kuri picks three times as many tiles out than Ping, and Ping picks out 24 tiles, how many total tiles are there? The area of the table is 19 inches by 5 inches. Will they have enough tiles to cover the tabletop?

   _____

2. The Miller family is redoing their garden. If they have a garden that is 500 square feet, and one side is 10 feet long, what is the length of the other side of the garden? If they plant 5 trees that need to be 5 feet apart and 5 feet away from the fence around the garden, will they have the space?

   _____

3. Bob is organizing his pantry. If he has cracker boxes that measure 2 inches wide and 10 inches long, how many boxes can he fit in one layer on a 30-inch-long shelf that is 4 inches deep?

   _____

4. You are packing picnic baskets for a day camp. Each basket needs to carry 8 square sandwiches, 8 apples, and 8 juice boxes. Would the most appropriate basket be an 18″ × 15″ × 9″ basket, a 72″ × 40″ × 18″ basket, or a 2″ × 6″ × 8″ basket?

   _____

5. Roberto wants to build a long train track. If each piece of track is 6 inches long, and he has 42 pieces, can he make a track that is 20 feet long? Can he make a track that is 22 feet long?

   _____

Name _____ Date _____

Reteach

5MG1.1, 5MG1.4

Area of Triangles

You can use a formula to find the area of a triangle.

Find the area of the triangle. Use the formula $A = \frac{1}{2}bh$, where
A = area, b = base, and h = height.

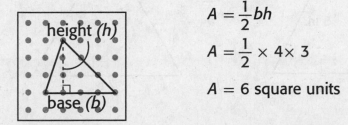

$$A = \frac{1}{2}bh$$

$$A = \frac{1}{2} \times 4 \times 3$$

$$A = 6 \text{ square units}$$

Find the area of each triangle.

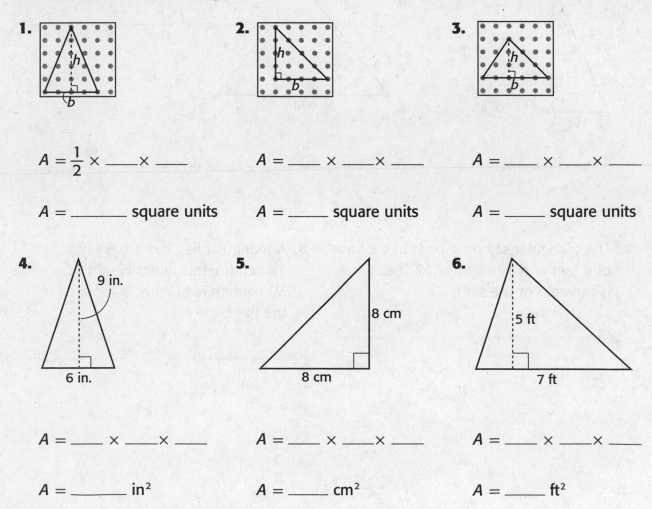

1.

$A = \frac{1}{2} \times$ ___ $\times$ ___

$A =$ _____ square units

2.

$A =$ ___ $\times$ ___ $\times$ ___

$A =$ _____ square units

3.

$A =$ ___ $\times$ ___ $\times$ ___

$A =$ _____ square units

4. 9 in. / 6 in.

$A =$ ___ $\times$ ___ $\times$ ___

$A =$ _____ in²

5. 8 cm / 8 cm

$A =$ ___ $\times$ ___ $\times$ ___

$A =$ _____ cm²

6. 5 ft / 7 ft

$A =$ ___ $\times$ ___ $\times$ ___

$A =$ _____ ft²

Skills Practice

Area of Triangles

Find the area of each triangle.

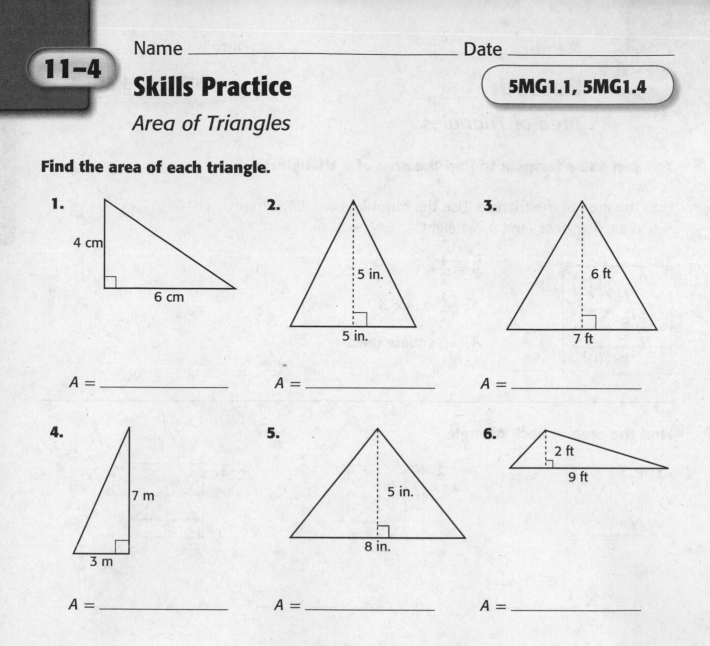

1.

4 cm

6 cm

A = _____

2.

5 in.

5 in.

A = _____

3.

6 ft

7 ft

A = _____

4.

7 m

3 m

A = _____

5.

5 in.

8 in.

A = _____

6.

2 ft

9 ft

A = _____

Solve.

7. The triangular sail on a boat has a base of 8 feet and a height of 12 feet. What is the area of the sail?

_____

8. A triangular flag has a base of 18 centimeters and a height of 30 centimeters. What is the area of the flag?

_____

11–5

Reteach

5MR2.3, 5MG1.4

Problem-Solving Investigation

Choose the Best Strategy

Alberto often goes along with his sister, Sonia, to videotape her soccer games. He records each $1\frac{1}{2}$ hour game. If she played 11 games, would Alberto be able to fit all her games on one DVD if each DVD holds 15 hours of video?

Step 1 Understand	**Be sure you understand the problem.** Alberto will videotape Sonia's soccer games. Each game is $1\frac{1}{2}$ hours. Sonia played 11 games. The DVD will hold 15 hours of video.
Step 2 Plan • Make a model • Draw a diagram • Look for a pattern	**Make a plan.** Choose a strategy. You can draw a diagram. Draw a line segment that is 15 inches long. Then mark intervals that are $1\frac{1}{2}$ inches long. Count the intervals to see whether you have 11 intervals. You can also use multiplication.
Step 3 Solve	**Carry out your plan.** Calculate how many total hours of video Alberto has. $1\frac{1}{2} \times 11$ games $= 16\frac{1}{2}$ hours of video Each DVD holds 15 hours, so $1\frac{1}{2}$ hours will *not* fit on one DVD.
Step 4 Check	**Is the solution reasonable?** Reread the problem. How can you check your answers?

Reteach

Problem-Solving Investigation   (continued)

Use any strategy shown below to solve. Tell what strategy you used.

- Make a model
- Draw a diagram
- Look for a pattern

1. Mitchell needs to buy enough paint to cover the fence in his yard. His fence is made up of 32 sections and he estimates that 1 gallon of paint is enough to cover 3 sections. How many gallons of paint would it take to cover his entire fence?

_____

2. Callie is throwing a party and spends a total of $135. She spends $20 on cake, $40 on food, and $25 for decorations. If the rest of the money was spent on music, how much did the music cost?

_____

3. Meredith is saving money each month to buy a car. In January, she has $100 in her savings account. In February, she has $125, and in March, she has a total of $150. How much money do you predict Meredith will have in her savings account by the end of October?

_____

4. Jordan works at a pool during the week. Monday he worked for 30 minutes, Tuesday he worked for 40 minutes, Wednesday he worked for 50 minutes. If the pattern continues, how long will he work on Friday?

_____

5. Roberto is looking for the better deal on a bag of pens. One bag has 6 pens for $3.65. Another bag is $4.98 for 8 pens. Which one should Roberto buy?

_____

Name _____ Date _____

Skills Practice

Problem-Solving Investigation

Use any strategy shown below to solve. Tell what strategy you used.

• Make a model   • Draw a diagram   • Look for a pattern

1. A pet store is building new cages for their birds. They have 8 cockatiels, 32 parakeets, and 28 finches. The different types of birds must be kept separate. How many cages will they need if each cage will hold either 2 cockatiels, 10 parakeets, or 14 finches?

_____

2. In art class, Aaron is drawing a symmetrical design. He draws a square with a perimeter of 120 inches. Then he draws another square inside of the first one that has a perimeter of 100 inches and then draws a square with a perimeter of 80 inches. What would be the perimeter of a fourth square if Aaron continues his drawing?

_____

3. Danielle picks fruit from her family's lemon tree. She picked 28 lemons. If each lemon makes $\frac{1}{2}$ cup of lemonade after adding water, how many cups of lemonade can she make?

_____

4. Adriana is making a dress. She has 5 feet of ribbon. She needs 12 inches of ribbon for the neck and two 6-inch pieces for the cuffs. How many cuts will she need to make to get 6 equal lengths from the rest of the ribbon for bows?

_____

5. Taye ran for 3 miles each week. On each fourth week, he ran an extra mile. How many miles did he run after 4 weeks? How many miles did he run after 7 weeks?

_____

Name _____ Date _____

Reteach

Volume of Rectangular Prisms

Volume is the amount of space a three-dimensional figure encloses. To find the volume of a rectangular prism, you can use a formula.

Find the volume of the rectangular prism. Use the formula $V = \ell wh$, where V = volume, ℓ = length, w = width, and h = height.

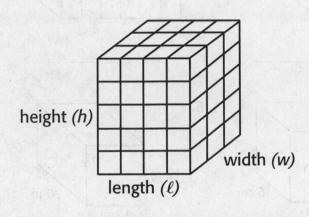

$V = \ell wh$
$V = 4 \times 3 \times 5$
$V = 60$ cubic units

Find the volume of each prism.

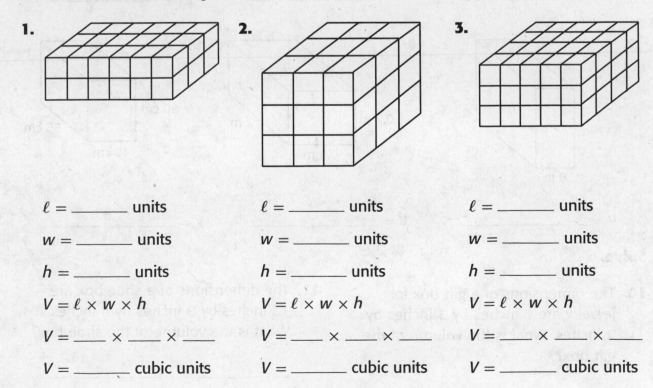

1.

$\ell =$ _____ units

$w =$ _____ units

$h =$ _____ units

$V = \ell \times w \times h$

$V =$ ___ $\times$ ___ $\times$ ___

$V =$ _____ cubic units

2.

$\ell =$ _____ units

$w =$ _____ units

$h =$ _____ units

$V = \ell \times w \times h$

$V =$ ___ $\times$ ___ $\times$ ___

$V =$ _____ cubic units

3.

$\ell =$ _____ units

$w =$ _____ units

$h =$ _____ units

$V = \ell \times w \times h$

$V =$ ___ $\times$ ___ $\times$ ___

$V =$ _____ cubic units

Name _____   Date _____

Skills Practice

Volume of Rectangular Prisms

Find the volume of each prism.

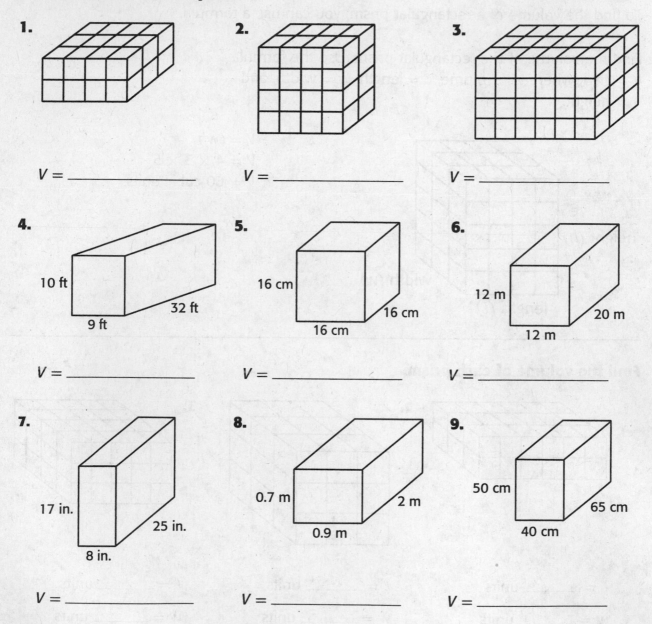

1.

V = _____

2.

V = _____

3.

V = _____

4.

10 ft   9 ft   32 ft

V = _____

5.

16 cm   16 cm   16 cm

V = _____

6.

12 m   12 m   20 m

V = _____

7.

17 in.   8 in.   25 in.

V = _____

8.

0.7 m   0.9 m   2 m

V = _____

9.

50 cm   40 cm   65 cm

V = _____

Solve.

10. The dimensions of a gift box for jewelry are 6 inches by 3 inches by 2 inches. What is the volume of the gift box?

_____

11. The dimensions of a shoe box are 13 inches by 9 inches by 4 inches. What is the volume of the shoe box?

_____